Wisdom from God's Garden

Bella Alex-Nosagie

Beauty4Ashes12:30 Publishing

Dallas, Georgia

Wisdom from God's Garden Copyright © 2014 by Bella Alex-Nosagie

All rights reserved. Printed in the United States of America. No part of this book may be used or reproduced in any manner whatsoever without written permission from the publisher except in the case of brief quotations for printed reviews.

For information contact:
Beauty4Ashes 12 :30 Publishing, LLC
Dallas, Georgia 30157
Beauty4ashes1230@aol.com
www.beauty4ashes1230.org

Unless otherwise specified, all scripture quotations in this book are from the Holy Bible, The New King James Version. © 1982 Thomas Nelson, Inc. Used by permission. All rights reserved.

Book Cover design by Angie Zambrano

ISBN-13: 978-0692293508

CONTENTS

Foreword vii

~Introduction~ viii

Part 1: 12 Petals of Wisdom

God Loves You so Very Much (If Only You Knew) 2

Trusting God is so worth It 6

What Is Your Special Name for God? 9

Good Morning. You Sleep Good? 11

Stop Trashing God's Treasures within You 14

You Were Born with Perseverance, Why Stop Now? 17

Don't Get It Twisted, You Are God's Champion! 20

Respecting the Magnificence of God 23

Helpers of Destiny 26

Givers and Receivers 31

Leaders and Followers 35

Why Wonder If You Have the X Factor? You Already Have the God Factor! 38

Part 2: 12 Flowers of Wisdom

Broken to Beautiful ………………………………….. 45

Do Not Fear Death …………………………………… 48

Prayerless You = Powerless You …………………………. 52

Don't Confuse Submission with Foolishness ………….. 57

Fulfilling Your Marital Destiny …………………………… 61

Women Arise! Do You Know You Are Royalty? ……….. 66

Lost in Translation …………………………………… 71

Loving in Spite Of …………………………………… 74

Sin is not Bigger than You ………………………………. 78

Self Examination is Absolutely Necessary ……………… 83

Seeds of Discontentment in Marriage …………………….. 88

Do Your Words Edify? ……………………………….. 94

Giving Your Life to Christ ………………………………. 98

I dedicate this book to my Lord and Savior Jesus Christ. The same yesterday, today and forever (Hebrews 13:8). The One who is, who was and who is to come (Revelation 1:8). You are the joy in my heart and the song on my lips. I worship you with all that is in me. Thank you Lord!

To my parents, Apostle Alexander Bamgbola and Rev. (Dr.) Grace Bamgbola. I want to thank you from the bottom of my heart for giving me a strong foundation in God. Thank you so much for your encouragement. Thank you for believing in me. Thank you for loving me. Thank you for praying for me since when I was a little child until now. Thank you for guiding me spiritually, physically and emotionally. I am so blessed to be your daughter. Dad, thank you for telling me to write a book. Thank you for also writing the foreword in this book. I love you very much. God bless you always and forever!

Foreword

I have had a rare privilege to go through this Holy-Spirit inspired book. I thank God for the life of the author, for putting this simple but greatly powerful book together under the guidance of the Holy Spirit.

God wants the author to get a most timely message across to His children who are in despair and battling with one trial/tribulation or another and overwhelmed by the issues of life. It is also an urgent message to those who are backsliding and those who are totally devoid of the knowledge of Jesus Christ.

The book contains in totality, a message of hope and the availability of the unfailing love of God. The love of God is ever-abiding and available to all. Receiving this message will turn the heart of any reader to God and give a deeper understanding as to walking with God in knowledge. As the author emphasized all through the book: God loves all and is seated upon His throne! I strongly recommend it to all. No one will read this book and remain the same again!

Apostle Alexander Bamgbola

ZION, The City of the Lord Ministries, Inc.

~Introduction~

God's garden is humankind. God created each and every one of us with so much love. The heart of His garden is marriage and family. It is in this garden that you will be blessed with so much wisdom as God teaches you how to navigate through the responsibilities of life as a spouse and a parent. We are all flowers in God's garden, but we mostly blossom or wither because of the families we come from or the families we make. This book is to encourage you to blossom. No matter how painful your past or present is, with God you can change your future for the better. God is the Unchangeable Changer!

Who am I? I'm someone who has basically been a Christian all my life. Today, I am a wife, and a mother to two wonderful gifts from God (a girl and a boy). I remember giving my life to Christ when I was six years old. As young as I was, something, which I now identify as the Spirit of God, propelled me to sing and join the choir of my local church. There wasn't a children's choir in my church then so I was privileged to be the only child singing in the adult choir. It was a place of discovery. That was when I discovered my love for singing. To this day it is my life's passion. I love singing, and if I could sing in my sleep I would. My parents are pastors. Over the years I have walked as a Christian, but to be honest, I haven't been a good Christian. Why? Because I came to a realization in 2012 when I reached the ripe age of thirty that I was not in love with God. I personally believe that you cannot be a good Christian if you are not truly in love with God. When you are in love with someone, you cultivate an intimate relationship. It is like a do or die thing. It pushes you, it overwhelms you, it takes you to a place of euphoria and you are willing to do *anything* to ensure that the relationship works. When I analyzed my life I recognized that I only ran to God when I had problems. In my daily life, I took Him for granted. Sometimes I would do my devotions/quiet time; many times I wouldn't. Intercessory prayer had always been a problem for me, despite growing up in a home where my mother was a valiant intercessor. It was just too intense for me, and I wasn't interested. Sure, I prayed, but never delved too deeply into spiritual warfare, which is a necessary component of the strength of a Christian. I had been doing things by my power and my might. God was not at the forefront of my life. He was not my priority as all other things were more important than the God who created me and gave me all I had.

So I guess God heard my cry because a year later in 2013, He took me to what I call "The Wretched Place". It's a place where God will take you out of love because you have been so blind to see how lost you are and how far away you are from His plans for you. Here, God will strip you down and break every pride in you. He will humble you and let you know you are indeed NOTHING without Him. It was painful, but has been the best lesson of my life. Also, I asked for it. Didn't I? I can now testify that I am absolutely, irrevocably in love with my God. I have repented and submitted every aspect of my life to Him. I had tried to make it on my own for thirty years and failed woefully. Sure, God had always been with me, but did I inquire of Him before I made decisions in my life? Yes, for the major things like marriage but not in every place else. When you are making decisions in your life, don't you inform your significant other and seek their perspective? Oh, I had been so lost, but thank God, not a lost cause! Now that I have submitted every aspect of my life to God, the journey to my purpose here on earth is beginning. My path to destiny has begun. See, every human being placed on this earth has a purpose. You cannot fulfill your purpose until you develop a close personal walk with God. You can come close because of God's grace on your life, but you cannot achieve all of His plans for you until you cultivate a deep and lasting relationship with Him. *For in Him we live and move and have our being, as also some of your own poets have said, 'For we are also His offspring* (Acts 17:28).

After the experience of "The Wretched Place," a writing ministry was born. "Beauty4Ashes12:30" is based on two scriptures — Isaiah 61 and Mark 12:30. It is about God's resurrecting love. Through this ministry, God is using me as a vessel to let you know if you are ever taken to that "Wretched Place" you are not alone. It is a testament to God's love for you. You will rise up from the ashes, greater and better than you ever were. Whatever you are going through is not as bad as you think. God loves you, and you are worthy of Him. God is on the throne. He sees all and knows all. He will always be there with you. There's no pain or burden you bear that He does not know about. He is looking out for you daily, and when you bring those burdens to His throne room, it gladdens His heart and He will move to lift you out of it. At the end of this phase, The Word of God shall be confirmed that truly, ALL things work together for good! *But seek first the kingdom of God and His righteousness, and all these things shall be added to you* (Matthew 6:33).

I am inviting you in obedience to God, to experience Him on a newer and deeper level. Beauty4Ashes12:30 is a place of rebirth. It is a place that shows the intense love that God has for us — His children. It does not matter who you are, where you have been, what you have done, where you are in your walk with God or if you know God at all. Come as you are, and partake of God's resurrecting love. You are most welcome! Happy reading...

The Spirit of the Lord God is upon Me, Because the Lord has anointed Me To preach good tidings to the poor; He has sent Me to heal the brokenhearted, To proclaim liberty to the captives, And the opening of the prison to those who are bound; To proclaim the acceptable year of the Lord , And the day of vengeance of our God; To comfort all who mourn, To console those who mourn in Zion, To give them **beauty for ashes**, The oil of joy for mourning, The garment of praise for the spirit of heaviness; That they may be called trees of righteousness, The planting of the Lord, that He may be glorified (Isaiah 61:1-3).

And you shall love the Lord your God with all your heart, with all your soul, with all your mind, and with all your strength.' This is the first commandment (Mark 12:30).

12 Petals of Wisdom

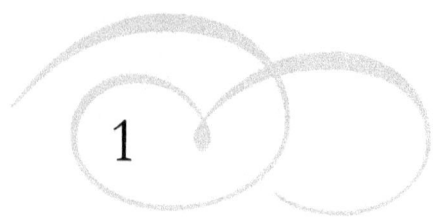

God Loves You so Very Much
(If Only You Knew)

'Call to Me, and I will answer you, and show you great and mighty things, which you do not know'

(Jeremiah 33:3).

What is a baby's first instinctive thing to do? Cry. This is their level of communication until they can talk. When my son wakes up, he cries to alert me that he is awake. Of course, this cry will escalate if I don't get to him fast enough. So what do I do to put his heart at peace? I start talking to him so he can hear my voice before I get to him physically. This quiets him down because he knows mommy is on her way to him!

So it is with God, who is a magnificent awe inspiring being, whose glory will be revealed when He comes back for His people, or if you die before His return, when you meet Him in Heaven. When life is throwing so many challenges and obstacles at you, cry out to God. He hears your cry and will answer. He will put you at peace even though you can't see him physically. He is always there. As you grow in Him, your level of communication will change from a baby, to a toddler, to a little child, to a teenager, to an adult, to a middle aged adult, to an aged adult, and so on. Walking with God is a process. Don't give up if He doesn't reveal Himself to you as you wish. It is a matter of time.

Let me give you an example. I have always wanted to hear from God, to hear His voice. Also, I have always wanted Him to show me visions and dreams. I have been a Christian all my life but I had never really surrendered all of my life to God. I still largely did things without running it by Him first. But I recommitted my life to Him and told him that I now wanted an intimate relationship with Him versus putting Him in the backseat of my life. Now I am finally hearing from Him, but it's not a conversation yet, which is the real level I want to get to. He drops words in my spirit from the Bible. In fact all the scriptures I use in this book are from Him. As I begin to write, He gives me words from His Word that establish the point I am making.

I love both my children but I relate to them differently. My daughter, who is my first child, is energetic and so was she energetic in my womb. I knew that someone extraordinary was coming. My son, who is my second child on the other hand, was very calm in my womb. No matter what I did to prompt him to move, he only moved when he wanted to and barely at all. I looked forward eagerly to ultrasounds to ensure he was alive and well. Outside the womb, he is a gentle soul compared to his very gregarious sister. He is, however, very strong and steadfast. My daughter is crazy about her daddy, and my son is crazy about me. As life goes on I will relate to them as a loving parent but counsel them based on their personalities and outlooks. As it is with God, He loves us all, but some are closer to Him than others. It is just the way it is. So if you want Him to be closer to you, you have to be crazy about Him. I can assure you that if my daughter is as crazy about me as she is about her dad, she will receive the very best from me. She already receives the best of me but she cannot get the very best or true essence of me until she is determined to be very close to me.

I say this because I've always been crazy about my dad but my relationship with my mom was iffy for the most part. I was born in Cambridge, Massachusetts, but raised by my parents in Nigeria until I returned to the U.S. for my college degree and corporate experience. Before I left Nigeria for the U.S., my mom and I had a heart-to-heart talk, during which she told me: "We have not always been close, I tried to do the best for you... It may not have come across well, but when you have your child, you will need me; it will be a chance for us to be close." I am crying as I write this piece because shortly before I got married in the year 2009, my mom had a devastating stroke! Tell me what daughter wouldn't need her mom on her wedding day, no matter what their relationship had been? When I had my daughter I couldn't look to my mom for help and encouragement because she was battling what stroke did to her. Her speech and reflexes had been weakened, and I could not look to her as a source. I regretted that I was never close to her when growing up! Please do not take God or anyone in your life who loves you for granted. Life is fleeting; make the most of it. Most importantly, you will get the most out of your life if you love God. He will teach you to love all, because God is love. *He who does not love does not know God, for God is love* (1 John 4:8). I use myself as an example to encourage you. I am no better than you; and so very far from being perfect. I strive however, to have a better relationship with God and I want you to do the same. Remember God loves you and He is on the throne!

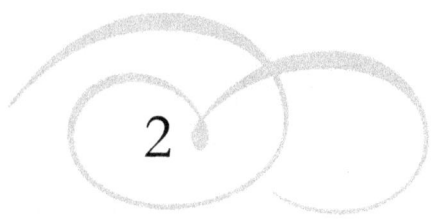

2

Trusting God is so worth It

"Before I formed you in the womb I knew you; Before you were born I sanctified you...(Jeremiah 1:5).

When my son wakes up for nighttime feedings he cries. As soon as I pick him up, he stops crying, but his mouth is busy moving with expectation. He knows exactly what's coming next — his food. As soon as he receives his food he relaxes in the crook of my arm and is absolutely content to eat to his satisfaction. This is what I find so fascinating and also hilarious. His eyes are closed! I find this hilarious because he wakes up with his mouth not his eyes and fascinating; because he trusts me so much to know I will feed him. Oh my Lord and my God, I praise you now and forever for showing me how utterly magnificent you are! *And my God shall supply all your need according to His riches in glory by Christ Jesus* (Philippians 4:19).

Do you know that there are examples all around you of how God loves and cares for you, but you will not see it until He "slaps you upside the head" to get your attention? The harder the slap, the more He wants to use you. *It is a fearful thing to fall into the hands of the living God* (Hebrews 10:31). Every day my two children show me just how much my Father in Heaven loves me. Mind you, it is only a glimpse of His love for me because God's love has greater depth than man's capacity to love. We can't fathom the depth of His love because there is really nothing to compare it to. This is why I love this scripture so much, *For I am persuaded that neither death nor life, nor angels nor principalities nor powers, nor things present nor things to come, nor height nor depth, nor any other created thing, shall be able to separate us from the love of God which is in Christ Jesus our Lord* (Romans 8:38-39).

To be honest, I was not inspired through my children about God's love for me until He took me to "The Wretched Place". Now my eyes have been opened and I am inspired through all kinds of people and things about God's love for me. I write to share it with you because as a fellow human, I know how the enemy messes with our minds to make us feel lower than bubblegum stuck on the bottom of our shoes. But we have all been delivered by His grace and a fire has been ignited in me to show you that God truly loves you, no matter what you think you have done. God's love is so merciful that if you can think of the most terrible person in your mind and that person gives his or her life to Him on their deathbed, or if a criminal does the same right before execution, he or she will be welcomed into Heaven. We should thank God every day that our God is not a man. If not, none of us will gain entry into Heaven.

God forgives all. No matter where you are in life, please come to Him. Maybe you walked with Him and left Him because you were discouraged or the pull of the world was just too exciting or maybe like me, lost focus and got distracted by life's responsibilities (which I happen to think is the most dangerous way to abandon God — you will have no idea when you start drifting and it may be many years before you realize it). Please, come back to Him. He is waiting with arms wide open. Trust in God, in Him all things are possible (Matthew 19:26). Meditate on the story of the prodigal son to feel some of God's love as you go about your day (Luke 15:11-32). Remember, God loves you and He is on the throne!

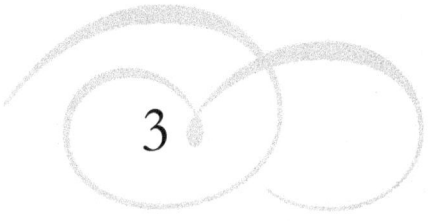

3

What Is Your Special Name for God?

And because you are sons, God has sent forth the Spirit of His Son into your hearts, crying out, "Abba, Father!" Therefore you are no longer a slave but a son, and if a son, then an heir of God through Christ (Galatians 4:6-7).

My parents are from Nigeria: a Yoruba dad and an Ibo mom. However, I do not speak either language, despite the fact that I spent the first seventeen years of my life growing up in Nigeria. Quite shameful, I know! At a certain point I went to school in the northern part of Nigeria where the language spoken is Hausa. Did I learn any Hausa? No, I did not. The only clear Hausa word I recall is abinci, which means food. Lord, have mercy on me! You have learned so far I have no affinity for languages. If you do, you are a blessed person indeed. Find a way to use this gift for God.

I can't speak Yoruba but thank God I can understand some of it and can pretty much follow in a conversation. My dad is often really touched when I address him as "Baba Mi", which means My Father. I don't address him like this all the time; I usually call him dad. I tend to call him daddy when I haven't talked to him in a while and I've missed him. But when I call him Baba Mi, he has a huge grin on his face. It touches him above other names. He knows I can't speak Yoruba so he appreciates my simple effort of addressing him with affection and respect.

What name do you call God? He has many names but what is your special name for Him when you enter into His presence? Just as you have terms of endearment for your loved ones, how do you affectionately address God your ultimate Father and ultimate lover? When you address someone affectionately, you automatically put them in a place to hear whatever you have to say favorably. When praising God, address Him affectionately. When repenting, address him affectionately. And above all, when asking, address Him affectionately. These will enhance your relationship with Him. *Oh come, let us worship and bow down; Let us kneel before the Lord our Maker. For He is our God, And we are the people of His pasture, And the sheep of His hand. Today, if you will hear His voice* (Psalm 95:6-7). Please read Romans 8:14-17 as confirmation, to see how special you are to God. No matter what you have been through, you are worthy of His love. Don't let the devil deceive you. You belong to God. Remember God loves you and He is on the throne!

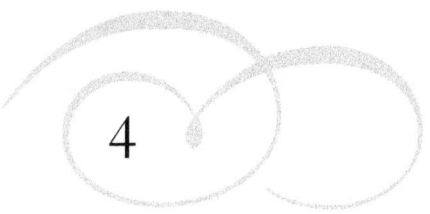

4

Good Morning. You Sleep Good?

Behold, He who keeps Israel Shall neither slumber nor sleep (Psalm 121:4).

"Good Morning. You sleep good?" This is what my daughter, when she was much younger, would ask her brother unfailingly every day. Not only in the morning but also every time he woke up from a nap. Sometimes she would wake him up deliberately just to ask him if he slept good! Ooooh! This used to get on my nerves because there's a lot I can accomplish when the baby is asleep. But after a while I noticed it gladdened my heart because it showed she was excited to have him around. She loved him and couldn't wait to interact with him. At this point, I came to a quick realization that I had never woken up and asked God about His day. I'd said "Good Morning, Lord" but I'd never inquired about His wellbeing. My children inspired me to start doing so immediately. Who says children can't inspire us? Mine definitely do. God is incredibly very busy taking care of us all.

I remember when I watched a movie called *Bruce Almighty*. Jim Carrey, a stellar comedic actor, played the lead. God was played by Morgan Freeman, another stellar actor. It got to a point Jim Carrey's character thought he could do God's job. Boy, was he overwhelmed real quick! His daily email inbox was filled with prayers from all over the world and he could not keep up. God is not a man. He is a divine, supreme being, and a lot of people demand His time. I make it a point that He is the very first person I speak to each day. So, tomorrow morning, why don't you ask Him, "How is your day going, Lord?" At some point, He will start to answer you. Just as my son will answer his sister when he starts talking, "Yes, Sis, I slept good." It will evolve to "Yes, Sis, I slept well."

I aim to be a friend of God just as Abraham was. God told Abraham to sacrifice his only son, the child he had waited for all his life. He obeyed without a question and knew that his friend, God, had a greater plan beyond his wildest imaginations (Genesis 22: 1-18). I want to trust God and walk hand in hand with Him, so that when any instruction or request comes from Him, no matter how senseless it may seem to my limited human mind, I will obey without a question and be so very blessed like Abraham was. Because Abraham obeyed, his seed is the most blessed seed on earth until this very day. He rewards those who diligently seek Him (Hebrews 11:6). Wives, you know how you welcome your husband home after his long day with a warm meal and ask about his day? God should be treated with such love and respect too. God does not eat; His food is Praise. So praise Him, converse with Him, and enjoy

Him. He's the best friend and lover you will ever have. God is the best. Oh, my heart rejoices in this love, which is now a mutual love. Let's pray for ourselves and the body of Christ that we will return to God and make Him our first love. Even though God's Word says the love of many will grow cold (Matthew 24:12), let's not fall victim to this. Let's spread this love. Remember God loves you and He is on the throne!

5

Stop Trashing God's Treasures within You

Let your light so shine before men, that they may see your good works and glorify your Father in heaven

(Matthew 5:16).

Have you ever thrown something in the trash that you thought you won't have need for again and then realized that you actually do need that something? If it is trash day and garbage has been collected, then you know that thing is gone forever. If you can purchase it, you will have to spend money to replace what was already yours in the first place. If it's not trash day, you will have to dig through dirt and stench to retrieve what you thought you would never need again. Neither option is appetizing. Why throw it away in the first place? That's how many of us are with the talents God has put in us. We don't appreciate them or we are unaware of them and so we trash them. Every human being was created to fulfill a purpose, Only if you walk closely with God will you have the direction to maximize your divine purpose. Talents, purpose and destiny go hand in hand. It is through the talents in you, that you will fulfill your destiny. Some of you may think there is nothing special about you and you are average. There is nothing average about God's creation. We were made in His image, *So God created man in His own image; in the image of God He created him; male and female He created them* (Genesis 1:27).

I have always known that singing is a gift that God placed in me. After recommitting my life to Him, writing became another obvious gift of mine. I've always enjoyed writing but never used it as an outlet to glorify God. This is what I will tell you — search yourself, review your five senses, review what motivates your heart, what stimulates your brain, what your hands like to do, what your legs like to do, what your body likes to do. Are you a flexible person? Are you an Athlete? Are you an Artist? Sculptor? Dancer? Carpenter? Teacher? Reader? Writer? Singer? Orator? Medical genius? What are you passionate about? What can you do easily even when your eyes are closed? Do you love to cook? Bake? Take care of the sick? Take care of children? Search yourself — there is something great in you that you have seen as a hobby or as nothing special. The most important thing to do next is to ask: "Dear God, how can I use my talents to move your Kingdom forward?" This is how you will begin to fulfill your Godly destiny.

There are many singers out there, but how many are using their voices to further the Gospel of Jesus Christ? Many started out in the church but because they were chasing money and fame, they decided to use their voices in secular music. You are in this world, but not of this world (John 15:19, Romans 12:2). Thank God, some have been convicted by the Spirit of God and are back to singing Gospel music today. This is why I used the term "Godly destiny". Do not use your talents to further yourself alone, but to further the Kingdom of God. If you are a Doctor for instance, God bless you indeed. Outside of the hospital, find ways you can be of help in your community. The best place to start using your talents to glorify God is in your church. From there, God will catapult you into your destiny.

Do not seek fame or riches; seek the will of God for your life. Many people will never be financially or materially rich here on earth. However, when we get to Heaven, and He says, "Welcome my good and faithful servant," you will know that there are no greater riches than your heavenly reward. Every gift or talent which God has placed in you is to be used for His glory and not yours. Jesus Christ was the son of Joseph the Carpenter. If you are a Carpenter, be a Carpenter unto God's glory. Whatever job you are doing, ensure that you are a light to others. Smile, treat people courteously, and be kind and willing to help. In this alone, you are glorifying God and moving His Kingdom forward. Please meditate on Matthew 25:14-30. It is my prayer that you are redirected from today on glorifying God with the talents which He has placed within you. Remember God loves you and He is on the throne!

6

You Were Born with Perseverance, Why Stop Now?

I can do all things through Christ who strengthens me
(Philippians 4:13).

If you spend a lot of time with children or when you become a parent, you will just have to admire God's work as an artist. He is an outstanding creator, of course, because HE is the Creator of all creation! When my son was almost seven months old, he did something that touched my heart and I began to thank God all over again for His love for me and blessing me with two precious children. His sister basically liked to play pranks on him because she knew that she was much faster being able to walk and run. When he would reach for a toy, she would grab it and throw it far from his reach. It never stopped him. He would crawl slowly with his little bitty muscles until he got to his toy. No matter how far she threw it, he would keep going until he retrieved it.

On this particular day my daughter ran up the stairs, assuming that her little brother wouldn't bother following her. After all, he had just started crawling three weeks before that day and was not quite fast yet. Guess what he did? He climbed the first step all by himself. I knew he was determined to get to her so I stood behind him so he wouldn't fall. There were a total of thirteen steps and he made at least ten all by himself! Anytime he faltered I was there to encourage him and help him up. At no time did he decide to go back down. He was focused on making it to the top just to be with his sister. I was so touched and inspired. God uses little children to teach us a lot of important things about life if we can discern.

We were all born with determination and perseverance. God created us to have these. Have you seen children trying to get to each milestone? They cry, but they don't stop. They must roll over, they must sit up, they must sit on their own, they must crawl, they must learn to stand, they must grow teeth, they must walk and so on. Each stage is so difficult, but they do not stop. They are focused on living a full life. God created it so. Remember you were a baby once so you have this perseverance in you. My son's goal was to catch up with his sister, because he wanted to play with her. He knew he was limited and wanted to ensure they played on the same terms.

What is your goal? What is your focus? Are you ready to do anything to achieve your goal? After deciding that I really wanted to know God and gave myself in total surrender to Him, He began to reveal Himself to me and I was led to change my goals from being earth-driven to Heaven-driven. I want to make Heaven, and I want to carry as many people as possible with me. God loves you. Please pick yourself up and rediscover the perseverance you were born with. You will rise from the ashes, but you must be willing to remove yourself from a piteous state. Just as I was behind my son as he climbed his Everest, God is behind you. Even when you fall down the mountain or you feel you can't go on, He is always there waiting with His loving arms wide open.

Please love God. His love makes loving worth it. Unrequited love is painful for a human being to go through, but God loves us even though we disregard Him and take Him for granted. *For God so loved the world that He gave His only begotten Son, that whoever believes in Him should not perish but have everlasting life* (John 3:16). Remember God loves you and He is on the throne!

7

Don't Get It Twisted, You Are God's Champion!

No temptation has overtaken you except such as is common to man; but God is faithful, who will not allow you to be tempted beyond what you are able, but with the temptation will also make the way of escape, that you may be able to bear it (1 Corinthians 10:13).

Have you ever laid down on the floor and given your baby free reign to crawl all over you and basically turn you into his toy or amusement park? It is so delightful. It is mutually enjoyable for both of you. I discovered the joy of this as a mother, and it is so much fun! My son's world is on the floor while mine is sitting on the couch. When I join him on the floor, I see his obstacles and I take away things that may be hurtful to him, which also enhances my relationship with him. He loves me more for joining him on the floor to crawl after him, roll with him, play with him in his world, and I enjoy rediscovering the child in me and the simple pleasures of life. From time to time, he sees my world. He'll sit with me on the couch or he'll join me on the bed, but always accompanied by me until he is old enough to handle the couch or the bed alone without falling. Then I will still be close by, but not as close as it is now because I know that he will be able to handle this by himself.

Where am I going with this? God relates to you at your level. He recognizes that not all His children are like the strong prophets of old Moses, Elijah, Elisha etc. Everyone has a starting point, and God is right there with you every step of the way. If God had taken me to "The Wretched Place" before He did, I would not have survived it. I would still be under a cloud of depression, anxiety and confusion. But He took me there at a time when my heart was ready to handle it because He had been preparing my heart for what was to come. It hurt, and I cried, but it did not cripple me. Rather, it empowered me. If not for "The Wretched Place" I wouldn't be writing today. Sometimes, something happens and you ask, why me? I can't handle this. But God's Word does not lie. You can handle it. You were created to be a survivor against all odds; you were born a winner! Out of all the sperm swimming in your mother's womb, you are the one that made it, took root, and came into existence. Don't ever think you are a loser. That is the lie of the enemy. You are a Champion! Trials come to make you stronger in God, not for you to wallow in pity and misery. Quite often, trials give birth to testimonies. Rise up, people! Rise up from the ashes! Just as you trust God when good things happen, trust God when the bad things happen. Focus on the end-goal and the big picture. *And we know that all things work together for good to those who love God, to those who are the called according to His purpose* (Romans 8:28).

Instead of asking, "Why me?" ponder on what God is doing in your life and how you can be better as a result of it. Pray, "Let your will be done, Lord; may I not get in the way of the great plans you have for me." It is normal to react in the flesh first because you are flesh, but ensure your spirit rises and praises God in the storms of life. When bad things happen, if you analyze it, God is taking you to a higher spiritual level — a place of breakthrough. He is maturing you, because you can't be a baby forever. Do you think when my son is in his twenties I will lie down so he can crawl all over me and drool all over me? No way! I can still lie down on the floor with him and cuddle, but that's about it. By then he will be a man, but I will always be his mommy. Mommies love cuddles and hugs no matter how old they or their children are.

Be encouraged. God has a great plan for your life but greatness comes at a price. Look at what precious stones including gold have to go through before they come out in their glorious state. Like them we need the fire of God to purify us, refine us and enable us handle our destiny. Remember God loves you and He is on the throne!

8

Respecting the Magnificence of God

For we do not wrestle against flesh and blood, but against principalities, against powers, against the rulers of the darkness of this age, against spiritual hosts of wickedness in the heavenly places

(Ephesians 6:12).

Praying is a solid way to grow in Christ. The wonderful thing about "The Wretched Place" is that an intercessor will be born in you. If you were never into spiritual warfare before, you will be now because God's reality check shows that your life is very spiritual. To be on top of the game, you will need to intensify your prayer life. The more I spent time in His presence with prayers and praises, the more I became astounded by the magnificence of Him. When you spend time in God's presence it's a place of healing, joy and enlightenment. *You will show me the path of life; In Your presence is fullness of joy; At Your right hand are pleasures forevermore* (Psalms 16:11).

I gave myself in total submission to God and told Him about things in my character which I did not like and asked that He should please purge me of them. I kid you not, I became almost immediately convicted about a lot of things. Let me try and describe it to you. Think of a buffet line that has all kinds of food. As you reach up to serve something unhealthy, a voice will caution you to put the serving spoon down. When you reach for something healthy, there is silence but also a feeling of peace that you are doing the right thing. Before while in prayers if my phone rang, I would pick it up because I took God for granted in not being able to see His magnificence physically. If you are at a board meeting do you pick up your personal phone when it rings? Or do you put it on silent and tell your secretary to hold all personal calls with instructions only to interrupt if it's a life or death emergency? If I know the President of the United States is coming to my neighborhood, I will ensure that I look my very best, be punctual, and make sure I behave properly with phones turned off and so on. I will do all this for a mere man, while with my magnificent God who created me, I just do whatever?

He has convicted me to make sure I don't touch my phone at all in His presence (no texting, no calling). Nothing is more important than Him. He has convicted me to the point that when I am praying and my children interrupt because of hunger or a diaper change or a potty break or anything, I say, "Lord, please excuse me," and I am singing all the way to the potty or while feeding the baby until I can resume intense prayers. I know a lot of Christians text in church I see it and I have been guilty of it. Thank God I have been delivered by His grace. No more phones. His throne is sufficient for me. Let your friends or family know when you are in church they will be unable to reach you until church is over. If there is an emergency, they will just have to physically come and inform you in church. When you give God the respect He commands, the windows of blessings over your life will be opened at a greater magnitude. When you are serious with God He will be serious with you.

My goal is to cultivate a deep relationship with God so that He will be my phone. If there is any emergency, He will tell me and permit me to go and take care of it. One thing that my faith knows is that nothing bad can happen if I am in His presence. If your faith is at a level where you are scared to turn off your phone in His presence, ask Him to help you trust Him that nothing bad will happen and commit everything into His hands. There is nothing God, our magnificent creator cannot do on our behalf. *But as it is written: "Eye has not seen, nor ear heard, Nor have entered into the heart of man The things which God has prepared for those who love Him"* (I Corinthians 2:9). Remember God loves you and He is on the throne!

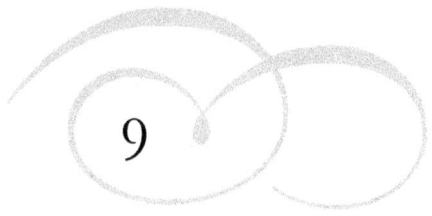

9

Helpers of Destiny

Peace I leave with you, My peace I give to you; not as the world gives do I give to you. Let not your heart be troubled, neither let it be afraid (John 14:27).

I love church for many things; not only for the empowering Word of God, but the sense of community and ability to socialize for a bit before heading back home. When you are in a place of love and acceptance, you want to bask in it before heading back to reality. The reality of life makes us too busy to catch our breaths, forever - hustling and bustling. Talking to my friends after church, I am able to catch my breath. There were times as a first time mom that I envied an Octopus. Sometimes I wondered why God didn't create additional appendages to sprout out of our bodies to answer all our baby's needs at once. This was when I had one child. Now with two I still find myself envying an Octopus. On this particular Sunday, I got to Church and dropped off my daughter in Sunday school. I had the baby in his car seat in one hand and the heavy diaper bag in my other hand, and I headed off to the main service. After a while he wanted out of his car seat so he was in my arms. I couldn't take notes because he wanted to take notes too. He was also very active so I basically had to hold him with two hands. By the time Service came to a close I was already worn out dealing with a very slippery and active baby. I headed off to Sunday school to pick my daughter up, and she protested she didn't want to leave and she got slippery too. So I had two slippery babies to hold onto plus the ever present diaper bag. I headed back to the main hall to talk with some key people I was already too worn out to socialize thanks to my children, but different people came up to me and said hi. It was finally time to leave. My son protested about getting into his car seat and my daughter ran off. With the diaper bag and now winter jackets I had to carry for both children, I knew I needed major help. I prepared to sit down and rethink my strategy because at this point the two hands I had were not enough to handle the children and all our stuff.

Do you know what this wonderful God we serve did? He sent a seven year old girl to help me. She just walked up to me and offered to help. She carried the diaper bag — quite a big bag, I must tell you — and the two bulky winter jackets, freeing my hands to hold onto my very active children. We headed out to the parking lot. We ran into her mother outside, who said she had been looking for her so they could go home. I thanked her mother profusely for raising such a sweet child because God sent her to help me. I kept looking away so her mother could not see the tears in my eyes. I was frustrated and overwhelmed, and in His infinite mercy He sent me a child to assist — a child with a heart of gold, as far as I am concerned. Her mother told me that she loves to help. I said, "Then she will always be blessed." When I end every chapter with the statement God is on the throne it is to let you know He sees all and knows all. Before I could open my mouth to ask someone to help, He sent me a child. I can't get over this, a child! God is able, God is awesome, and God reigns supreme. When you grow in Him, His favor increases upon your life. When you pray in your heart and simply say, "Lord, I need help!" He will send help. When you have a sense of urgency to serve God and fulfill His call on your life, pray and ask Him to send your helpers of destiny. You need help to get from zero to hero in His Kingdom. Jesus had a destiny to fulfill even though it was not palatable to his flesh at a point He asked his father to take this cup of suffering from Him but yet was still nice enough to say let your will be done not mine (Luke 22:42). Oh, how Christ hurt for us.

There are different kinds of destiny helpers. Some will not be aware that they are sent to help you, but they are strategically placed by God to help you. *As they were going out, they met a man from Cyrene, named Simon, and they forced him to carry the cross* (Matthew 27:32). Even the soldiers who were mocking Jesus were compelled to find someone to help Him carry the cross. Simon of Cyrene was a destiny helper. Another destiny helper was Joseph of Arimathea, a wealthy disciple who gave up his own tomb for who he recognized as the Messiah (Matthew 27:57-60). Joseph could not prevent the death of Jesus but he did what he could to honor his Messiah. Joseph of Arimathea was aware he was a helper because he made a conscious effort to do something. Recognize that every human being is unique. Some humans are in very painful situations, but out of their pain their destinies will be fulfilled. Fulfilling destiny is not rosy at all. There are thorns along the way, and some people are in a constant state of pain. Some people have debilitating illnesses, some people are handicapped or disabled, but out of what the world will see as shortcomings, they will thrive and fulfill their destinies. Setting up charities, bringing awareness to the disease, ministries are birthed — all kinds of positive things occur in the midst of their pain.

Be prepared in fulfilling your purpose to meet obstacles, rejection, hurt, and pain just like Jesus did, but focus on the end result. Stay prayerful and connected to God. He will send you many Josephs and Simons to help you. There are also some helpers of destiny that will provoke you into fulfilling your destiny. These are Pharaohs. Some people are just so mean and evil to you, and you wonder why. They push you into a tight corner and you feel you can't breathe. But from that tight corner you will break free and move to the next step in fulfilling your destiny. Fulfilling your destiny requires you to face adversity head on and to turn it into something positive.

Jesus fulfilled His destiny because He looked at the big picture. It was for the benefit of all mankind and was not about Him or how He felt. His was true unconditional love. May God keep us all not to get sidetracked and to seek His face constantly for encouragement, comfort, uplifting, and direction. If you are stuck and overwhelmed, prayerfully call your helpers of destiny forth. There are some people who will be unable to sleep until they help you. Yes, God touches people's hearts to that point. Pray also for the ability to recognize your helpers, that pride or shame will not prevent you from accepting help. We are too blessed to be stressed! Remember God loves you and He is on the throne!

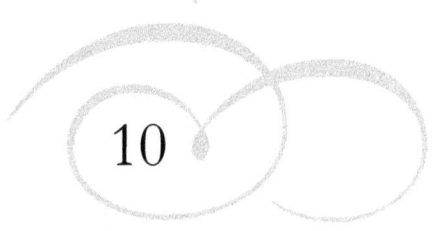

10

Givers and Receivers

"Listen! Behold, a sower went out to sow. And it happened, as he sowed, that some seed fell by the wayside; and the birds of the air came and devoured it. Some fell on stony ground, where it did not have much earth; and immediately it sprang up because it had no depth of earth. But when the sun was up it was scorched, and because it had no root it withered away. And some seed fell among thorns; and the thorns grew up and choked it, and it yielded no crop. But other seed fell on good ground and yielded a crop that sprang up, increased and produced: some thirtyfold, some sixty, and some a hundred." (Mark 4:3-8).

Are you more of a giver or more of a receiver? Some people are generous to all; some like me have been conditionally generous - meaning that at the root of it, we are more receivers than givers. Even though I've been a Christian for many years, basically all my life, I discovered after going through "The Wretched Place" that I had been more of an Old Testament Christian than a New Testament Christian. I practiced a lot of "an eye for an eye". I was basically nice to you if you were nice to me. If you were mean, I would avoid you and be mean too if I couldn't take it anymore. I was judgmental and quite "Holier than thou". It became very clear to me after my wretchedness that without the grace of God, I was nothing. Who was I to feel better than others or sow seeds of meanness because people had been mean to me? I admitted to myself that I had not been a good Christian. I asked God to touch me in all areas and show me His way, not mine. Each day I am inspired by His revelations and it gladdens my heart that a change is happening within me.

I have been a conditional giver to humans. If you get me something, I'll get something for you. If you don't, see ya later. I'm so glad God has saved me. What an embarrassing and immature way to view life. *He who is faithful in what is least is faithful also in much; and he who is unjust in what is least is unjust also in much.* (Luke 16:10). If you are a giver, your financial situation will never influence giving. Having a generous heart does not mean you have to be wealthy. I asked God to deliver me from being a conditional person, and He led me to a couple of scriptures to understand unconditional love and the blessing behind giving. It is important to understand that when giving to God, it is an act of faith. Many times I was prevented from giving a generous offering to God because I calculated how much I wanted to have left for me after paying all my bills. There is a blessing attached to giving. Now I'm not saying that you should go and empty your bank account and give all to God because you know He will triple it. Everyone is at different spiritual levels. If this is what you are convicted to do and your faith can carry it, kudos to you. When you are a giver or a generous person, you will be hurt time without number because people will take advantage of you and use you. This was another thing that prevented me from giving. If you are strong in spirit, please continue to be generous. Don't worry about how people respond. Do your part and let God do His part. And His part is awesome! Please note that giving does not have to be monetarily alone. You can give your time, your skills, your heart, etc.

When you give, think of yourself as a farmer. Farmers plant numerous seeds. Many times they don't even remember where they have planted seeds. Crops germinate at different times. Some grow faster than others. Some seeds will die and not reproduce. Some seeds will simply get lost. Some seeds will flourish, and during harvest time you will be laughing all the way to the bank. People evolve over time just as things evolve over time. You may help someone in need today, but tomorrow you may be the one in need and this person you helped previously will be in a position to help you. However, make sure that you give unconditionally, because some people you've helped along the way will pretend you don't exist when the tables turn. However, I promise you God will always raise someone up, something up or a situation up to give back to you generously. His Word says it, *Give, and it will be given to you: good measure, pressed down, shaken together, and running over will be put into your bosom. For with the same measure that you use, it will be measured back to you"* (Luke 6:38).

When God rewards your faithfulness for sowing unconditionally, it's in the overflow. God's bank is limitless. When your seeds mock you, He will always be there to make sure you never lack. The more you give, the more you will receive from all kinds of people and places and things. It is a way to increase God's favor upon your life. If I have to choose between wealth and the favor of God, I will choose His favor. God's favor is limitless and can take you from wretchedness to dining amongst Kings. So brothers and sisters, be encouraged. Where you give and people take advantage of you, take your hurts to God. He will heal you and reward you. When you give, give as unto God and not unto men. God will reward you, not men. It is God who touches the hearts of men to give back to you. Not every earthly seed that you sow will give you an earthly harvest. Some people may not have much in the physical but in the spiritual realm, they are majestically wealthy.

There is a life after this - eternal life with Jesus Christ if you have given your life to Him. Everything you do has physical and spiritual consequences. Stay in God, do your best and He will do the rest. Remember God loves you and He is on the throne!

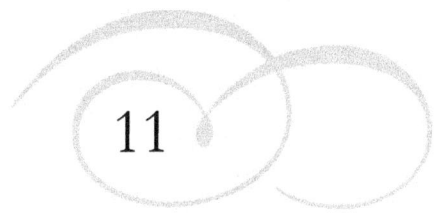

11

Leaders and Followers

Let this mind be in you which was also in Christ Jesus, who, being in the form of God, did not consider it robbery to be equal with God, but made Himself of no reputation, taking the form of a bondservant, and coming in the likeness of men. And being found in appearance as a man, He humbled Himself and became obedient to the point of death, even the death of the cross (Philippians 2:5-8)

To be an excellent leader, you must be an excellent follower. I know it sounds weird, right? Because there is always a clear distinction in our world about leaders and followers. It's almost like you have to choose sides. If you are not a leader, then you are a follower. But many great leaders you see were and still are great servants/followers to others. Christianity is love and acceptance of all people. Sometimes Christianity may not make sense to our human selves. I mean, if someone hurts you, it's only logical to hurt them right back. But when you grow in Christ, you will learn about unconditional love and forgiveness.

Christianity is about being Christ-like. Jesus Christ never repaid hurt with hurt. He humbled Himself to live amongst His creation and submitted to their insults and brutalities. You cannot attain unconditional love on your own. Humans are just not programmed that way. We are greedy and selfish. Unconditional love cannot exist where greed and selfishness abide. By submitting to God and cultivating a meaningful relationship with Him, the ability to love unconditionally and serve unconditionally will come upon you. This is not an overnight journey because a baby does not turn into an adult overnight.

The higher you go spiritually the more you will be able to subdue your flesh. If you have a problem with anger for instance, the more you spend time with God and work on your spiritual life, the sooner you will notice that the triggers that were guaranteed to make you lose your temper do not work anymore. Working in corporate America for many years under all kinds of managers, I quickly realized that the best managers were the ones who had no problem leaving their comfortable, well-designed offices to go down in the trenches and work with those in cubicles or even all the way to the hole in the wall warehouse to figure out a solution. These were the managers who I admired and looked up to as role models. Many of their colleagues preferred to troubleshoot from their offices. The open door policy never really seemed like the door was sincerely open. You are more able to identify with someone of authority who comes down to your level than someone who issues instructions from the comforts of above. So it is with

Christianity, God resists the proud and gives grace to the humble (James 4:6).

The day God elevates you to a position of authority, you must remember your roots and that you were not always on top. Remember the services you had to render to make it to the top. Becoming a leader should make you even more of a servant. Because you are now in a position of authority, people will look up to you and emulate you. Set a good example, teach the up and coming about humility and service so that when they become leaders tomorrow, they will know how to do so effectively. Spend time reading the book of John and see what our Lord Jesus Christ left behind. His comfort zone in Heaven and came down to earth to be one of us. He loved all of us so much that He never turned anyone away. At the end of it all, He died a brutal death. But thank God, He rose again — still teaching, encouraging and serving. Best of all, He left the Holy Spirit for us. If the Holy Spirit is strong in you, you will live a life of service, no matter what leadership heights you attain.

The best leaders are the best followers. To be a great leader you must have a teachable spirit and the heart of a servant. Many times the people you are leading have wonderful knowledge to disperse. If you are proud and unapproachable to learn from your followers, you have failed as a leader. Be a Shepherd and make yourself available to your flock. Don't be too busy to lend a helping hand. May God give us the grace to have hearts of servitude. Remember God loves you and He is on the throne!

12

Why Wonder If You Have the X Factor? You Already Have the God Factor!

Therefore we also, since we are surrounded by so great a cloud of witnesses, let us lay aside every weight, and the sin which so easily ensnares us, and let us run with endurance the race that is set before us, looking unto Jesus, the author and finisher of our faith, who for the joy that was set before Him endured the cross, despising the shame, and has sat down at the right hand of the throne of God (Hebrews 12:1-3).

I used to love watching the show X-Factor while it aired in the U.S. All kinds of people from age twelve upward were encouraged to audition and chase their dreams as singers. At the season finale, one person out of the thousands who auditioned would win a five million dollar recording contract and a commercial deal with Pepsi. Then there was the declaration of having the X-Factor, which was that special and effortless star quality, that made the winning contestant stand out from the rest. In one of the episodes, a sixty-nine year old pastor who looked and dressed like Santa Claus auditioned. At the age of sixty-nine, you would think he would be on some porch somewhere, swinging and basking in retirement but this elderly gentleman came on the show, sang his heart out and went through to the next round. He still believed in chasing his dream, even though he was in the later years of his life. God accepts you as you are. The devil will tell you that it's all over, but God lets you know that as long as you are alive, there is hope. *Let everything that has breath praise the Lord...* (Psalm 150:6). As long as you have life in you, it is not too late to fulfill your destiny.

I was talking with my dad one night and he confirmed what has been a heavy burden in my heart. He told me it has been said the graveyard is the wealthiest place on earth and therein lies so many unfulfilled destinies. If all the dead could wake up and fulfill their destinies, I believe this world would have been a much better and positive place. Let me make it clear that the devil has his own destiny too, and he is fulfilling it very well. Do you want to help further his cause of taking as many people as possible with him to his eternal home of hell fire and brimstone? Or do you want to be on the winning side, the blessed side, the Godly side? We are in the end times, the battle lines have been drawn. The world is getting much more terrible and it will not get any better. Jesus Christ is coming back soon. Are you sure that you want to continue on a Godless path, pouring all your energies into this temporary place? Look unto *Jesus, the author and finisher of our faith...* (Hebrews12:2). The devil makes things look so appetizing and offers many short cuts, but these short cuts will cut your life short. Do you want to end up in the grave like many others without fulfilling your reason for existence?

You are here for a divine purpose. You have the God Factor! He has put so much in you, but you will have no clue how globally gifted you are, until you tune in to God's channel and submit your life to Him. Would you prefer having a parent that lets you have your way all the time or a parent that teaches you right from wrong and how to live a life of integrity? The devil is like a dysfunctional parent. Don't get caught up with him because he will not prepare you for life but totally destroy your life. God is our ultimate Father and He chastises those He loves (Hebrews 12:6). *But the very hairs of your head are all numbered* (Matthew 10:30) means that He cares about your wellbeing. It means that you are unique and special, just by your very existence. So I urge you, brothers and sisters, to wake up. Time is ticking away. Now that you know God loves you irrevocably and you have the God Factor, what are you going to do about it?

I will tell you how I'm doing it. I am getting on my knees and thanking God daily that He saved me from hell on earth and also eternal hell. I am giving myself to Him in total surrender. I am telling Him to activate every talent which He has put in me and to create avenues for me to share with the world and move His Kingdom forward. I am transforming myself physically, emotionally and spiritually through fasting, exercise, meditating on God's word and warfare. And things are already happening in my life to the glory of God. I also had an epiphany recently and have found God and I are on the same page. The amount of intense physical training soldiers in the U.S. military go through is beyond my scope of mind. They are also subjected to medical exams to ensure they are physically fit to defend the U.S. So how can I say I am a soldier in the Lord's army and look like a jelly donut? I've struggled with weight for so many years, and I have had so many ups and downs. Now with the Lord on my side I know I can't fail. Ask any expert — weight loss begins in the mind. If you have not conquered the love of food in your mind, you are wasting your time. I asked God for help in this area and He let me know all things are possible in Him (Mark 9:23). We must be physically fit to be in the Lord's army. Look your best, feel your best, do your best, and let God do the rest. Remember God loves you and He is on the throne!

12 Flowers of Wisdom

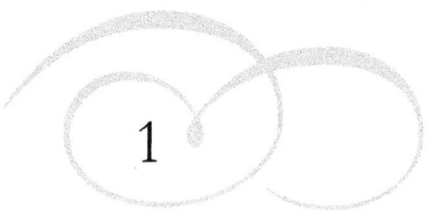

1

Broken to Beautiful

And you shall love the Lord your God with all your heart, with all your soul, with all your mind, and with all your strength.' This is the first commandment. And the second, like it, is this: 'You shall love your neighbor as yourself.' There is no other commandment greater than these" (Mark 12:30, 31).

It's funny how life is, where in the midst of joy there is also pain. My son was born in 2013, and it's the only reason I cannot write off the year as a hot mess. He is definitely a special child because it was during my pregnancy with him I realized I was dissatisfied with my spiritual state. I wanted to be in love with God. I was a Christian and grew up as a Christian, but I was in many ways a baby Christian. I prayed about this, and it took almost a year for God to answer my prayer. He did in an explosive way. I was literally brought to my knees. I was taken to "The Wretched Place". I was broken and I was humbled. The words fail me to express how the very foundation of me was shaken. Of course when bad things happen, there is always that question, why? And God began to reveal Himself to me. He had to break me to use me for His glory. He had to break me so I could see how awesome He was. He had to break me so I could stop compartmentalizing Him and instead give Him free reign in EVERY facet of my life. He had to break me so I could begin to fulfill my God given destiny. I wept. I wept about my brokenness and wretchedness. I wept asking Him to forgive me for if He had not done this I wouldn't have known how lost I was. God had to break me in order for me to see His immense love for me. God had to break me to move my focus from earthly things to heavenly things. I was reduced to ashes, and God began to make things beautiful again.

From this brokenness, He showed me His love and taught me to show love to others. He used a couple of people to point me in a new direction of sharing His love. He also spoke to my heart to share this love and an author was born. I just want to thank God for His faithfulness and loving me enough to call me to attention. I always knew I was called to do His work, but through this brokenness He activated the call urgently on my life to encourage people that He exists. Even in the midst of pain He is orchestrating something beautiful for your life. God allows you to be broken so you can draw closer to Him. So you can really be still and know that He is God (Psalm 46:10). Life and its responsibilities can be so distracting, but He put you on this earth for a purpose and I am glad that He loved me enough to break me and activate His call on my life. To make Him my first love. To work hard and urgently to further His Kingdom. To be used as a vessel to encourage others who are wallowing in their brokenness.

Rise up from the ashes and return to God. Find strength in God and know that all the pain ends in this life. It will not follow you into eternity. This pain is to help others who are going through it, how can you be a testimony if you've never been tested and, more importantly, overcome? This pain is to help you attain a higher spiritual level because only by attaining a higher spiritual level will the troubles of this life never paralyze you or your faith in God.

When you walk with God, be ready for anything. Babies have it good, don't they? When they want to sleep, they have a bed to lie on. When they open their mouths before they even cry out, food is placed in it. They have everything they need. But as they grow older and eventually become men and women and the responsibilities of life occur, life gets harder. So it is in the spiritual realm. When bad things happen and things get tough, don't get angry with God. Instead hug Him tighter and love Him harder because only God can get you through the storms of life. However the year is for you, remember God loves you and He is on the throne! He sees all, knows all and is aware of everything. Don't put Him in the backseat. Allow Him to be the pilot of your life. With God on your side you can never fail (Romans 8:31).

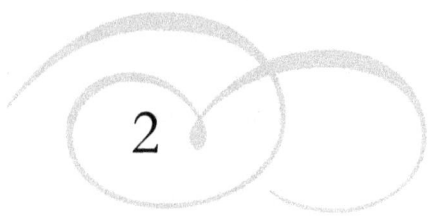

Do Not Fear Death

For God has not given us a spirit of fear, but of power and of love and of a sound mind (II Timothy 1:7).

I've always hated flying. I developed a phobia for it when I was about twelve years old. This evolved into a general fear of heights. I don't like ladders, elevators, sky scrapers or anything that takes me up. When I used to fly quite frequently for a previous job, I would check the size of the plane before reserving a ticket. The smaller the plane the more anxious of a traveller I would be. Smaller planes are highly susceptible to turbulence. Before I get on any plane I pray. Not just any prayer. You know the prayer you pray if you know death is around the corner? I confess every sin I can think of. I ask the Lord for His mercy and to receive me into His bosom if the plane crashes. I lay hands on the plane just as I am about to enter it and plead the blood of Jesus over it. I pray from take off to landing, anxious and never at peace because a plane can crash anytime. If I happen to be given a window seat I keep the window shade closed all through. I don't want to look down and remember I am up in the sky with nowhere to run if anything goes wrong. Lord, have mercy on me!

His word says perfect love casts out fear (1John 4:18). God is love, and if you have Him in you there is no reason to be afraid. I have given all my fears to Him, and He is changing my outlook on life to be strong and courageous in all things. When further analyzed, I have been quite afraid of dying. I have been a Christian all my life but scared and wondered if my name was in the Book of Life. I wondered if I died, would I truly go to Heaven? Death is certain. We will all die, but where you will spend eternity is determined by whether you give your life to Christ or not. Truly letting go of the old man and moving your focus from satisfying your flesh to satisfying your spirit (Ephesians 4:22-24). *Jesus said to him, "I am the way, the truth, and the life. No one comes to the Father except through Me* (John 14:6). I thank God that when I went through "The Wretched Place" He broke me and transformed me for His glory. I actually laid flat on the ground and surrendered every area of my life to Him and told Him, "Here I am. Send me. I am all for you now." One thing I noticed immediately was I was free from the fear of death. I knew if I died I would go to Heaven, and for the first time in my life I was a 100% sure. Praise God!

What a relief to let such fear go. But a new fear took over. It is a positive fear that keeps me in check. I don't want to die and go to my Lord empty handed with no works to show what I did in His name, for His glory, and to further His Kingdom. If I am afraid of death today it's not because I am not sure of where I will spend eternity, but because I want to make sure I fulfill my purpose and complete the work my Father created me to do before He calls me home. *And He said to them, "Why did you seek Me? Did you not know that I must be about My Father's business?* (Luke 2:49) Jesus was a very serious young man. He knew he had a destiny to fulfill and got right down to business in thirty-three years of life and only three years of ministry. Look at all He accomplished. God is awesome! When you are busy for God, count it all joy. God has given all of us a certain number of years to live on this earth. Let me give you an example. Let's say He has given you fifty years to live and you give your life to Him at age forty. If you walk with Him closely and take Him very seriously He will reveal your purpose to you. In those ten years that you are unaware you have left, God will begin to create so many avenues for you to further His Kingdom. Don't be worn out. Embrace it fully because His love for you wants to ensure you do not die and meet Him empty handed. He wants to reward you for your faithful service.

I have some questions for you. Are you prepared for death? Is your heart in good standing with God? Are you living for Him and seeking His face for ways to further His Kingdom? If you die today are you a hundred percent sure that you are going to Heaven? My friends, let's not be afraid of death. We will all die. It's for certain and only God knows when. Let's live for Him, let's connect with Him, let's put Him first so we don't miss it. If you want to give your life to Christ today or recommit and give God free reign in EVERY aspect of your life please follow the steps outlined at the very end of this book. Remember God loves you and He is on the throne!

Do not lay up for yourselves treasures on earth, where moth and rust destroy and where thieves break in and steal; but lay up for yourselves treasures in heaven, where neither moth nor rust destroys and where thieves do not break in and steal. For where your treasure is, there your heart will be also (Matthew 6:19-21).

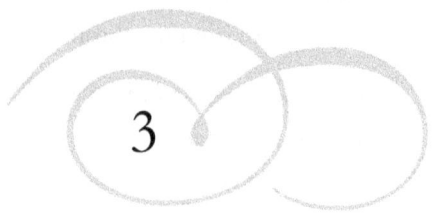

3

Prayerless You = Powerless You

Therefore take up the whole armor of God, that you may be able to withstand in the evil day, and having done all, to stand. Stand therefore, having girded your waist with truth, having put on the breastplate of righteousness, and having shod your feet with the preparation of the gospel of peace; above all, taking the shield of faith with which you will be able to quench all the fiery darts of the wicked one. And take the helmet of salvation, and the sword of the Spirit, which is the word of God; (Ephesians 6:13-17)

I've always loved to sleep. Seriously, sleep and I have been best friends for several years. In fact living in the U.S. for fifteen years now, I am still getting used to the climate here (I doubt I will ever be used to it). Growing up in Nigeria we had year round summers and rainy days but no fall or winter. I loved sleep so much that my grades in college were usually better in the spring and summer time than in the fall and winter time. I loved sleep so much that when I had my daughter and was introduced to the wonderful world of sleepless nights as a new mother, I found myself crying so many times with the baby.

Not because anything was wrong, but just because I wanted to go back to bed and sleep. I have loved sleep so much that getting up to pray at night or in the wee hours of the morning has been a lifetime problem. In retrospect, I placed so much importance in sleep that I am quite ashamed of myself. It got to the point that I would get so upset with my husband for waking me up to ask a simple question. We sleep differently. I have quite a busy mind so it takes me a while to find sleep. When I do, any interruption messes me up and to find sleep again is not easy. He, on the other hand, can sleep off easily but if you wake him up, he's ready to go to the grocery store and buy a gallon of milk. I'll just be drowsy and angry if you wake me up, grizzly bear angry. Thank God for His grace.

One important thing I've learned from "The Wretched Place" is sleep is not an asset to attaining a higher spiritual level but a detriment. Sleep will hold you back from fulfilling your destiny. Sleep will enable the enemy and all his cohorts continually plague you and make your life miserable. Sleep will keep your life stagnant. Sleep will keep you in an average place. Sleep will keep you as a follower and never the leader of the pack. Sleep will make you a Jack of all trades but a master of none. Sleep will lead to eventual spiritual death. Of course we all have to sleep as humans but we should not prioritize sleep. Love of sleep is a subtle destroyer and keeps you in a passive state versus a proactive state. *How long will you slumber, O sluggard? When will you rise from your sleep? A little sleep, a little slumber, A little folding of the hands to sleep— So shall your poverty come on you like a prowler, And your need like an armed man* (Proverbs 6:9-11).

Do you see what God has saved me from? By enabling me fall in love with Him, sleep is no longer a priority. When do you think I spend most of my time writing the contents of a book? When do you think I spend most of my time in intercessory prayer and spiritual warfare? Being a Christian is serious business. When you are asleep you are in a state of unconsciousness. Only the grace of God keeps you to wake up and see another day. Do you think the enemy is happy you are in Christ and are Heaven bound? Satan wants you to go to hell with him. That's why he has made this world so appetizing to distract you. But you will not miss it in Jesus' name. Amen. Wake up to the tricks and lies of the enemy. He is a big distraction to fulfilling your Godly destiny and making it to Heaven. When is the majority of evil deeds conducted? In the dark, in the deep, dark cover of night. We cannot afford to prioritize sleep. Would you like to wake up and find someone holding a knife to your throat or a gun to your head? So it is in the spiritual realm. A Christian without prayer is a Christian without power.

There are different kinds of prayers. Right now, I am referring to spiritual warfare. This is when you get on your knees in the dead of night putting on the "full armor of God" and unleashing ground breaking prayers on the powers of darkness. Please don't misunderstand me. Spiritual warfare can be conducted at anytime, but at night is an effective strategy against the countless evil plans of the enemy. *Be sober, be vigilant; because your adversary the devil walks about like a roaring lion, seeking whom he may devour* (1 Peter 5:8). Also, God's mercies are renewed every morning (Lamentations 3:23). Wouldn't you like to partake of those mercies first thing in the morning? Many people queue up overnight waiting to purchase the latest technological gadget or whatever crazy deal or discount is going on in the stores. I would rather sacrifice my sleep and spend it in the presence of God. When you start your day in battle mode there is NOTHING the enemy can do to take you down. Starting your day in warfare already negates every evil plan of the enemy against you for the day. Praying in the spirit strengthens your spirit and chases anxiety and fear from your life. Pray daily like your life depends on it because guess what? Your life depends on it. Prayer is what will move mountains out of the way in your life. Prayer is what will move you from ordinary to extraordinary. Prayer will remove you from the status quo and make you succeed in what may seem to be a saturated market. Prayer will also make you succeed where others have failed.

Warfare is where you charge yourself up to face and divert the evil plans of the enemy. Warfare is what will make the enemy tremble in fear when strategies are being planned to make you fall. Or do you think you are not discussed in the enemy's camp? Every child of God is discussed just as there are tactical units in the US military to bring the enemy down. So are there units in satan's camp to tear you down daily. James 5:16 talks about the "effective prayer of a righteous man". There are all kinds of prayers, but many times effective prayers can either be attained or maintained in warfare. Every Christian needs to be a prayer warrior. It is with spiritual warfare that positive changes occur in your life and surroundings. Gone are the days you deliver your requests to the prayer team to pray for you and rely on their prayers alone. No one knows your need the way you do. No one can explain it to God the way you can. So stop diverting prayer requests to the prayer team and going home to sleep. Ask the prayer team to pray along with you, not just for you. There is a prayer warrior in you. If God can raise an intercessor out of me, ex-lover of sleep, He can do the same for you.

Brothers and sisters rise up. Good things in life don't come easy. Heaven is the best place to spend eternity but the enemy is going to do all he can to prevent you from making it there. The more you are on track for fulfilling your destiny the more satan and his cohorts will come after you. You need to spend time in spiritual warfare. Take yourself to the point where the enemy sees you as a general in God's army. He will have no choice but to bow and proclaim you a lost cause. There will be nothing he can do to take you to hell with him. Only spiritual warfare can take you to this point. *that at the name of Jesus every knee should bow, of those in heaven, and of those on earth, and of those under the earth, and that every tongue should confess that Jesus Christ is Lord, to the glory of God the Father* (Philippians 2:10-11) Let's put down our sippy cups as baby Christians and get right down to business! Time is ticking away. Yesterday is gone forever and cannot be lived again. Remember God loves you and He is on the throne!

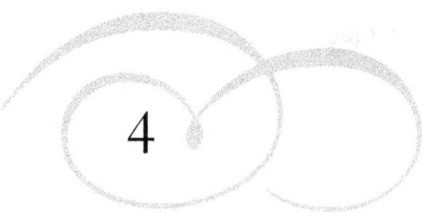

4

Don't Confuse Submission with Foolishness

Wives, submit to your own husbands, as to the Lord
(Ephesians 5:22).

I am from a culture that values respect highly. The more respectful you are, the more you are shown favor. From a young age, children are taught to respect their elders; greet them respectfully and address them respectfully. I am the only girl in my family, having three brothers — two older and one younger. I understand men a lot because I grew up surrounded by men. Of course with their different personalities all men are not the same, but there are some basic traits all men share. No matter what part of the world you reside in, men value respect over all. In fact, men equate love with respect. If you want a man to love you, you must respect him. If you disrespect him continually or disregard him, he will walk away and settle down with someone who values him. This is why the Bible commands wives to submit to their husbands (Ephesians 5:22-24). However, this is what I truly want to discuss. In reviewing my life and discussing with my friends, we women are guilty of doing something, and it must be addressed. In obeying the word of God we submit to our husbands, but submission should not be done foolishly. The same Bible that tells us to submit tells us to be wise as serpents but gentle as doves (Matthew 10:16). Women will do anything for love. We can quit our jobs and move from civilization to the back woods all for love. Women are guilty of putting their dreams on hold because of love. Career-minded women who were driven with goals to get to the top of the corporate ladder will marry and become mothers and say motherhood is now their dream. One day you will wake up and discover you have lost yourself. The man you put your life on hold for will die eventually. The children who are now your dream will grow up and leave you to pursue their own dreams. Every human being was placed on this earth for a divine purpose. Don't be so totally focused on your family that you let go of yours. Don't get me wrong, being a wife and a mother is a gift that should be treasured and enjoyed. You are fulfilling a purpose already, but there is more to you than being a wife and a mother. I should also quickly add here that your dreams should never be at the expense of God or the family He has gifted you with. The focus should always be God, family and everything else. However, don't put things on hold because you are overwhelmed or satisfied with things as they are. Instead ask God to help you balance it all.

Many women in the name of submission have lost themselves because they are trying so hard to please, respect their husbands and keep a peaceful home. Then the children come, and the women are stretched even more trying to balance husband and children. One day you will be like me and look in the mirror, not recognizing who you have become. When you are a woman of substance and a woman with dreams and goals you are pursuing, your husband will value you more read Proverbs 31. She is not a lazy woman by any means. She takes care of her family, but is also a resourceful and working woman. Remember your husband is your life partner; submission does not mean you lose yourself and become his slave. A slave does not have a voice. A slave obeys the master and suppresses desires and needs. Many of us women feel our husbands won't support our dreams so we wallow in despair and make him and the children our dream. You are not your husband's slave. A wife should be valued over all other women — that's why he married you in the first place. Many wives get married and relax. The difference in courtship is that men chase women, but in marriage women maintain the chasing. In other words if you want him to keep chasing you, it's up to you. We now need to empower ourselves and keep things interesting. If you wear wigs, instead of having just one, buy different distinct styles and switch things up so he doesn't know which glorious version of his wife will appear. Be physically fit, spiritually fit, fashion conscious. Let your husband be proud to take you out and flaunt you. Keep your sweet personality. Be loving always, but do not in the name of submission suppress the essence of you. Be driven. Also, be all you can be. Be a praying woman. This is the key to keeping your home in good standing with God, your husband and your children. Instead of being angry with your husband and creating a hostile environment, forgive him and hand him over to God. God created him; God can change him. Commit yourself also to God to remove attributes that will not mesh with your husband's and your destiny. If your husband is away from you because of work, business or some other reason, instead of being depressed that he is away and crying like a baby rise up and use this as an opportunity to transform yourself for the better. Ensure that he returns to an asset not a boring same old story.

Women are powerful mystical creatures. We are the ones that reproduce. Every man on this earth came from a woman's womb so don't make yourself a doormat for any man. Respect men, but ensure you know you are powerful in your own right and remember to respect yourself. There is a saying that behind every successful man is a woman. This is very true, but also behind any downtrodden man is a woman. What are you using your female power for? Are you enhancing your husband, your home and your environment? Or are you tearing down your husband, your home and your environment? Find yourself, find the power in you and the best way to do this, is to spend time in prayers and communion with God.

My sisters, I wish you all the best in life. Let us be joyful, engaging, vibrant, elegant, God-fearing creatures so we can impact our home and those around us positively. Make yourself a catalyst for positive change. Meditate on Proverbs 31:10-31. Remember God loves you and He is on the throne!

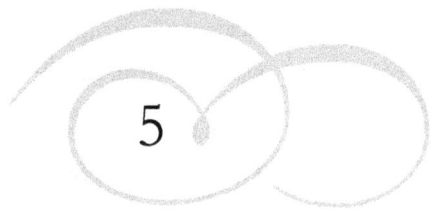

5

Fulfilling Your Marital Destiny

Therefore what God has joined together, let not man separate (Mark 10:6).

I can't tell you how many books I've come across talking about how wives should pray for their husbands. It is preached in churches to pray for your husband before he arrives and even more so after arrival. I watched an interview on the very respected and global evangelist Billy Graham. Just after he celebrated his 95th birthday he was asked how he handled temptation from the opposite sex all through his ministry. His answer was simple and also full of depth and maturity. "By never being alone with a woman," he said. He always made sure he had a witness in the room when ministering to women. We hear the term Man of God all the time, but I'm here to tell you that you should not forget the word MAN in that statement. No matter what great heights of ministry your husband reaches, the devil is always on the look out to jump on him and make him fall. And the quickest way to make a man fall is through a woman. Men are wired differently from women. Women fall in love with their ears, and men are visual. You get and keep their attention by looking good. You get and keep women with words of love and endless affection.

I have always been fascinated with the dynamic of male and female relationships. Even before I got married you would find me at couples seminars to equip myself for the future. Men and women are so different, yet God created us to be one. I have been married as of today for four and a half years, Those of you who have been married for many more years I'm sure will have a load of wisdom to impart. Shortly before our fourth anniversary, my husband left for military duties, and I began to find the strength within me. Many of the things he took care of, I began to take care of. I'm the only girl in my family and my daddy's princess. I grew up in an atmosphere of love and support. I've always been taken care of. I entered marriage with those same expectations, looking for even more security, affection and to have every need met. I didn't factor in that my husband's background is very different from mine and that he did not grow up the way I did. He is street smart, and me? I'm what I call princess smart —just a teddy bear who loves to love, be loved and be pampered. So the conflicts began because I couldn't understand why he did not see things my way and he didn't understand why I did not see things his way. In the middle of all this we were blessed with two beautiful children and had many happy moments and bad moments too, like all marriages. When he left I determined he would not return to the same woman physically, emotionally or spiritually. I started to ask God for guidance and He opened my eyes to a lot of things. Instead of questioning why my husband and I are so different and clashing over it, why don't I look to Him for the beautiful design He has for us to fulfill our marital purpose?

When you look to God for guidance, all those differences that drive you and your spouse crazy will begin to make sense. I recently came across a book called *The Five Love Languages,* and a lot of things began to make sense. According to the author Gary Chapman, there are five languages of love: quality time, acts of service, physical touch, words of affirmation, and receiving gifts. I can tell you right now that my husband primarily views acts of service as love; cooking, cleaning, taking care of the house. I view gifts, physical touch and words of affirmation as love. This goes back to how we grew up. The funny thing is my husband is a better cook, better cleaner and better housekeeper than I am. So how do we move forward? Through prayers, heart to heart talks, reading books and attending seminars that enrich marriages.

Husbands, I hope you are praying for your wives. Because we need it big time! You know those women that have five children yet manage to have their nails and hair done, makeup in place, house clean, ability to give every child the attention they need, and so on? I call them Super Women because I am not one of them. I have only two children under the age of four, and many days I think I'm going to lose my mind! Prayers are very necessary on both sides in marriage. The Bible says we are a helper (Genesis 2:18) meaning we should help build him up and support him and guide him to where he needs to be.

The Bible commands men to love their wives as Christ loved the church and gave His life for it (Ephesians 5:25), which denotes a sacrificial, unconditional love. This is very hard to do without God's help so husbands in turn should find out what their wives need to feel loved and secure and do their best to meet it.

Performance management is very necessary in marriage just as it is required in corporate America to keep your job and get promoted with bonuses attached. Don't be afraid to ask your spouse, "How am I doing?" You can work as hard as you can and think you are a good spouse, but if you do not check in with your spouse from time-to-time, you are wasting your time. Perhaps your method will work for someone else's spouse, but the key is to find what makes your own spouse tick. Let us love each other and empower each other. Be a strength to your spouse and be an asset also.

God created marriage to be a joyful union, a place of peace and love. And yes, God wants the fires of romance to continually burn. He created sex and endorses it within the confines of marriage. *Let your fountain be blessed, And rejoice with the wife of your youth. As a loving deer and a graceful doe, Let her breasts satisfy you at all times; And always be enraptured with her love* (Proverbs 5:18, 19). Don't get too busy or overwhelmed that you neglect each other sexually. Remember the MAN in the Man of God statement. Even a Christian man is wired for sex because he is a man first and will remain a man until he is given his celestial body after death or during the rapture, whichever comes first. So many women think because they are doing the work of

God or busy with career and kids their husband will understand if they slow things down in the bedroom. That's the opportunity the devil is waiting for. Be all the woman you can be. Look good, be supportive, be there for your husband in the bedroom and in all aspects of life. No element should be neglected in marriage that's why we constantly need God's help to be successful in it. Let's determine to improve our marriages today from good to better from better to best and also from bad to good. Remember God loves you and He is on the throne!

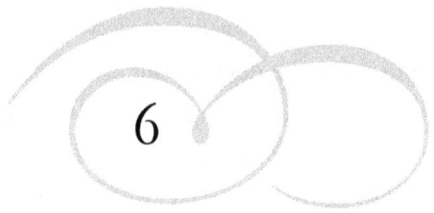

6

Women Arise! Do You Know You Are Royalty?

But you are a chosen generation, a royal priesthood, a holy nation, His own special people, that you may proclaim the praises of Him who called you out of darkness into His marvelous light; (I Peter 2:9)

My insight into womanhood so far? I never really appreciated womanhood and what it is to be a woman until I became a mother. When you have a helpless little being looking at you for life, sustenance, guidance, nourishment and love, the inner strength and super strength in you will emerge. Being a wife and a mother and a woman who loves God, I have to encourage my fellow women. Women are so strong and so blessed and able to overcome the most devastating circumstances yet many of us behave as victims and walk with our heads down because we allow men to define us instead of looking to God for our definition. *For in Him we live and move and have our being, as also some of your own poets have said, 'For we are also His offspring'* (Acts 17:28).

So many women are crying. Many of us are walking around with plastic smiles on our faces. Many women are saying, "How did I get here? This isn't me. This isn't the life I envisioned There's got to be something more than this." And, yes, there is. God's love and a deep abiding relationship with Him will unlock the joyful essence of you. Women are so special to God. Look at how He made us and blessed us to be capable of so much. When I began to meditate on womanhood and what it means to be a woman, I discovered there are three things that occur in our lives to bring us fulfillment and completion and turn us from girls to women: we were created to have a period, to have sex and to have babies. If any of these three are lacking in your life, there is an identity crisis.

I know if you have been having your period for several years now you may be so over it. But think back to the days when you were expecting it when all your female peers were having theirs, one after the other, and you wondered when yours would appear. It is the first rite of passage that you are a woman.

God created sex to occur within marriage. God created us to yearn for a lifelong committed and intimate relationship with a man. In God's natural order of life, marriage was created to fulfill the yearning He places in each woman's heart for a lifelong male soul mate. *For this reason a man shall leave his father and mother and be joined to his wife, and the two shall become one flesh'; so then they are no longer two, but one flesh. Therefore what God has joined together, let not man separate* (Mark 10:7-9). This is why for women it gets to a point just like waiting for your period to arrive you begin to wonder when it will be your turn to get married. Your peers begin to get married and there is anxiety, especially once you start thinking of your biological clock. Marriage is God's ticket to having sex. It is for pleasure and for procreation. Sex is sacred and is God's gift to marriage (Proverbs 5:15-19). As pleasurable as sex may be, it comes with a responsibility. This is why it is the second rite of passage for a woman.

Having sex means you are ready for the responsibility it comes with, motherhood! Having a baby is the third rite of passage of fulfillment as a woman. When a woman is barren she is devastated. It's like you are not given a membership card to an elite and exclusive club. This is far worse than waiting for your period to arrive or even wondering when you will be married. Suddenly you can't relate to conversations anymore. You feel you stick out like a sore thumb as you appear at numerous children's parties, huge present in hand but with no children in tow. You have no idea what it's like because the only way to understand motherhood is to be a mother. And you cry, and you hurt, and you wonder why. My sisters, love God. He's the only one that can wipe the tears from your eyes. He's the only one that can give you peace. He's the only one that can assure you even if you find yourself lacking in womanhood, He loves you and you are woman enough for Him!

Each rite of passage into womanhood requires blood to be shed. We are sacrificial beings. And who can understand us more than Jesus Christ Himself, who sacrificed His life for mankind or God Himself, our loving Father and Creator who gave His son to die for us. Being a sacrificial being makes us sacrifice continually in our daily lives in all kinds of ways, but what ends up happening is we forget that even though Jesus Christ sacrificed Himself on the cross, He rose from the dead in three days! Do not have a victim's state of mind but wake up to the victor and overcomer that you are. Women are deep mystical creatures. Do not underestimate your worth and the power in you. We are the backbone of creation. We are the ones who populate the earth. Is it any wonder the enemy attacks and tries to break our spirits? There are so many of us wounded and broken, but God is not through with us yet. Rise up and take your stand! Be strong! Be vibrant! Be a positive catalyst! Be a woman! Being a woman is a good thing, God made it so.

And the Lord God said, "It is not good that man should be alone; I will make him a helper comparable to him (Genesis 2:18). We were made to intercede and be a helpmate for mankind. There is a prayer warrior in you. You go to battle on your knees and to receive strength to meet all the demands of life. We were created for the good of mankind to be a blessing from generation to generation. Your definition and identity is in God. Do not let any other human being devalue you or make you feel worthless. God loves you no matter how sordid your past is. Give your life to Him and let Him use you to impact the world around you. Why is there a prostitute in the genealogy of Jesus Christ? (Joshua 2; Matthew 1:5). Jesus Christ could have chosen to keep his earthly bloodline impeccable but He chose to be descended from the imperfect, including a prostitute. Don't feel guilty and feel that you are not worthy. God loves you unconditionally.

Anytime you feel down remember you are a daughter of a King and not just any King, the King of Kings! Hallelujah! It does not get any more royal than that. Walk tall, hold your head up and fulfill your destiny. Tune out the devil and his mind games and whoever he uses to tear you down, male or female, and focus on God's love and purpose for you. You were born to be a blessing so be a blessing to those around you. Encourage each other and walk in love. Remember God loves you and He is on the throne!

7

Lost in Translation

In this manner, therefore, pray: Our Father in heaven, Hallowed be Your name. Your kingdom come. Your will be done On earth as it is in heaven. Give us this day our daily bread. And forgive us our debts, As we forgive our debtors. And do not lead us into temptation, But deliver us from the evil one. For Yours is the kingdom and the power and the glory forever. Amen
(Matthew 6:9-13).

I'd been teaching my ten month old son to say mommy. He started saying "mmmm" which evolved to "meh" and then "ma-ma-ma-ma." He didn't say "mama"; he just sang "ma" repeatedly. I had been so focused on teaching him to say mommy because that's what I wanted him to call me that I almost missed the fact that he was actually addressing me as "mama." When he would get hungry or upset or want to cuddle he would crawl to me, hold on to my legs and pull himself up, stretching his chubby little hands up to me saying, "ma-ma-ma-ma" like a song. I thank God for His grace for bringing me to realize this.

How many times are we so focused on a goal that we miss the joys in life or we fail to tap into the true success of the goal? How do we pray to God? Do we lay prayers with wrong motives at His feet or do we ask that His will be done? Many times God speaks to us and has answered our prayers, but we miss it because He does not answer as we expect.

In my prayer time I have been asking the Holy Spirit for prayer points. Many of us pray, but our prayers can miss the mark because we are not praying properly. Sometimes when you are angry with someone, you can find yourself praying vengeful prayers. Sometimes you may want something or someone badly because you believe that's what's best for you and this is what you pray for. I'm sure many of the female readers can relate to the following example. You see this cool, fine, church-going brother and you ask God to give him to you as a husband, but God sees his heart. You do not. God knows who will complement you and enable you to fulfill your destiny. In asking God for a spouse, don't ask God for somebody you believe is good for you; ask God for who He believes is good for you and who He has created for you *But the Lord said to Samuel, "Do not consider his appearance or his height, for I have rejected him. The Lord does not look at the things people look at. People look at the outward appearance, but the Lord looks at the heart* (1 Samuel 16:7).

Our prayers should be God-motivated and not self-motivated. I had to go back to the Lord's Prayer and meditate on it. I still continue to meditate on it, asking the Holy Spirit for insight and clarification. I don't want to spend my time praying superficial, self-seeking prayers, I want to pray prayers that touch the heart of God. It is important to ask that God's will be done when you pray. Make your requests known to God, but also pray that His will be done. Recognizing that He is the Alpha and the Omega who knows the end from the beginning, who knows the best for you, who has the best in store for you. Prayer is letting go and letting God take over. Another important line in the Lord's Prayer is, "And forgive us our debts, As we forgive our debtors". If you want God to hear your prayers and also forgive you, make sure you have forgiven. *For if you forgive men their trespasses, your heavenly Father will also forgive you. But if you do not forgive men their trespasses, neither will your Father forgive your trespasses* (Matthew 6:14, 15).

Whenever you want to check the motives of your prayer go back to the Lord's prayer and meditate on it. Ask the Holy Spirit for guidance and direction. Remember God loves you and He is on the throne!

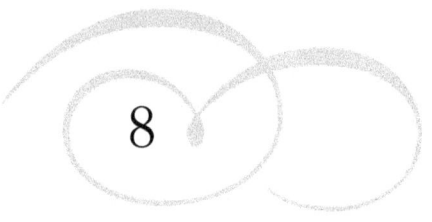

8

Loving in Spite Of

Therefore, my beloved, as you have always obeyed, not as in my presence only, but now much more in my absence, work out your own salvation with fear and trembling; for it is God who works in you both to will and to do for His good pleasure. Do all things without complaining and disputing, that you may become blameless and harmless, children of God without fault in the midst of a crooked and perverse generation, among whom you shine as lights in the world, holding fast the word of life, so that I may rejoice in the day of Christ that I have not run in vain or labored in vain (Philippians 2:12-16).

I'm always stressed when heading out of the house because I love to be punctual, but somehow with two children I never make it. After having children, punctuality flew right out of the window. I don't care if I start preparing four hours before, I will still be late to wherever I am going. It's so disheartening for me because punctuality has always been a part of my identity. I mean, you know the stereotypical woman who takes forever to get ready? Not me. Growing up with all men in the household, I was never the girl who would cause unnecessary delays. I wanted to be part of the action and if I wasted time, I got left behind. So I learned to be punctual, never late. But here's me in the future with two children and unable to make it on time. Talk about stress, irritation, anxiety. It all came down to a yell, an ungodly yell.

It was a rainy day, a dreary day, and I had to get to our Christmas carol rehearsal on the other side of town. The wipers of my car aren't working. This is my first solo performance in four years. I'm a perfectionist. I want everything to go well. I want to represent God. I want to glorify Him with the gift He has placed in me. I am also nervous; I have butterflies in my belly. I always get nervous when all the attention is on me, but I've missed singing. It's like breathing, and it's a talent God blessed me with. How can I hold myself back from serving Him and blessing the world with what He has put in me? I am stressing out big time! My sister (Referring to my brother's wife since you are aware in previous posts I am the only girl in my family) offers me her car but she's running late I know traffic is going to be a mess. I am stressing. My daughter starts to act up. She's in the No-No-No stage. To get her to do anything these days is so dramatic I don't have time for this so I yell at her. I yell at her real good and she starts to cry. I don't care for her feelings because there's baby number two to contend with. Finally when we are on our way, stuck in traffic and being lifted by music from my best friend (a friendship that transcends space and time so Soul Sista will be a more appropriate description) I have time to examine myself and I ask God to forgive me. *Examine yourselves as to whether you are in the faith. Test yourselves. Do you not know yourselves, that Jesus Christ is in you?—unless indeed you are disqualified* (II Corinthians 13:5). I turned into someone else, someone mean and angry because I was stressed. A dark side came out of me and I was embarrassed by it. I said, "Lord this is not who I want to be. Help me to be patient and to stop stressing." He then reminded me of His unconditional love and how I am required to practice it as a true reflection of Him.

We all have different sides. There is darkness in all of us. Only the light of God can purge us. I was reminded of how I had judged people before because I reacted to their negative attributes and drew away. They may have just been having a bad day like me, but their attitude turned me off and I distanced myself from them. If any of you had seen me yelling at my daughter like God did, you may not like me or even want to know me. Before, I was the Christian who treated people the way they treated me. If you were absent-minded where I was concerned, I would ensure I was also absent-minded about you even though I was very aware of who you were. I was such a pretender. I thank God for showing me what a fraud I was as a Christian. He is teaching me to love even when I am not loved, and it is refreshing, It is a better outlook on life because I am sowing good seeds regardless of whether the seeds come back to me. There are different sides to people good sides and bad sides. Positive traits and negative traits only the grace and mercy of God can renew us and change us.

I just want you to know that practicing unconditional love is necessary. It is how to be, it is how to live, it's what Christ did when He died on the cross for us, and it resides in you and me. If we are His people and we follow in His example we need to stop being hypocritical, full of pretense and judgment. The church is to be a place of sanctuary, but unfortunately it's where a lot of hypocrisy and judging goes on. We are all sinners saved by grace. We should extend this grace to others. In our homes, outside of our homes, when we meet people, we should remember we represent Christ and therefore should love the way He loves. I really thank God for "The Wretched Place" He took me, to break me down and make me a new creature. I now understand a lot of things. I pray for His will always whether I like it or not. I submit to it and I am being blessed daily.

When you show God you trust His decision making skills He does more and more and more for you. He continually covers you in His favor and love. It's awesome! Let's examine ourselves and be better Christians. Let's ask for God's light to expunge the darkness in us. He is the light of the world after all. *Then Jesus spoke to them again, saying, "I am the light of the world. He who follows Me shall not walk in darkness, but have the light of life* (John 8:12). Remember God loves you and He is on the throne!

9

Sin is not Bigger than You

What shall we say then? Shall we continue in sin that grace may abound? Certainly not! How shall we who died to sin live any longer in it? Or do you not know that as many of us as were baptized into Christ Jesus were baptized into His death? Therefore we were buried with Him through baptism into death, that just as Christ was raised from the dead by the glory of the Father, even so we also should walk in newness of life (Romans 6:1-4).

I was doing laundry one day. And you know when you have been working hard all day and you take care of that final task with a sigh of relief so you can go relax and put your feet up? Well, I tossed all the dirty clothes in the washing machine, glad to complete the final household task for the day. When the washing cycle finished, I opened up the machine expecting to see clean clothes that I could toss into the dryer. I was in for a bad surprise. Somehow the little box of fabric softener sheets had been tossed in with the clothes so there were sheets intertwined with clothes and wet strips of the carton were also intertwined. Since I had unknowingly added a foreign matter into the washer, the washer had still done its job to provide clean clothes; however the foreign matter had made those clean clothes really dirty. I ended up taking out the clothes, shaking them out, cleaning the washer to remove all evidence of the dryer sheets and tossing the clothes back in so they could be washed again. What should have been a straightforward task became a long and tedious task.

This is how many of us are when we let sin rule us. Sin can be deliberate and sometimes unconsciously we err. Sometimes we think we have let things go, but they are stored deep in our hearts. See yourself as a washing machine. When you ask God for forgiveness, He washes your sin away during the washing cycle. When the cycle is complete, it is over and done with. He forgets about your sin. But are you ready to let the sin go? If someone has hurt you, have you truly forgiven the person? What about yourself? Sometimes things happen and you are so angry with yourself for being made a fool of. Have you forgiven yourself or do you keep reliving it day after day? I read recently that forgiveness is a choice, not because you have forgotten but because you have made a choice to not let the misdeed rule over you. Forgiveness is unconditional love. It's the way God loves us and is how we should love one another, including ourselves. Forgive those around you who have hurt you and caused you pain, and also forgive yourself.

If we are truly God's children and seek to love Him and do His will, when we sin we should be uncomfortable because we know our Father in Heaven disapproves. We should repent and ask Him to help us keep away from that sin. Returning to that sin is like eating vomit and that's gross! When we find ourselves tempted to repeat that sin again we should run to our Father for help versus running away from Him and succumbing to the sin because we know He will forgive us anyway. Sin causes distance between God and us. Many of our struggles today can be traced back to sinful decisions we made because we pushed God away and wanted to prove ourselves right. Taking God and His grace over us for granted is a mistake many Christians make today. The fear of God is lacking in this generation. *Jesus Christ is the same yesterday, today, and forever* (Hebrews 13:8). God is the same. He has not changed and will never change. He is still the same God who opened up the ground so the complaining Israelites could be swallowed up. He is the same God who let the Red Sea cover Pharaoh and his Egyptian army who were in pursuit of the Israelites. Because we now reside in the dispensation of grace and Christ came and died for us we think we can continue to sin because God will always forgive. God is not a fool. Going back to the same sin you have supposedly repented from makes you look like my washing machine did on that unforgettable laundry day. You may feel good with yourself that God has forgiven you, but you are still unclean and in a woeful state.

As long as we have these bodies of flesh, sin is always around us. We should not let sin rule us. We should let our love and respect for God rule our lives. Then you will not be eager to compromise your faith. You may tell yourself, "God will understand. It's how things are done these days." Fornication and adultery are rampant in the church, Christians are living together without being married, atrocities and all kinds of abominations Christians are doing believing God understands. Beware and be very careful because God has the same expectations for us whether or not the times have changed. He still expects us to chase after righteousness and holiness daily. *For the kingdom of God is not eating and drinking, but righteousness and peace and joy in the Holy Spirit* (Romans 14:17). God will not be mocked or made a fool of. If you could see Him and His magnificence, would you take Him for granted? I am not perfect. I struggle daily especially when God exposes the ugly parts of me. But one thing I notice is the closer I get to Him, the better I become. He prunes me to glorify Him. Pruning can hurt because it's difficult to stop doing things the way you always have, but the power of God makes it possible. You know how it is when children run away and hide because they know they are doing something you disapprove of? That's how we are with God, hiding our sin and shame away because we don't want to disappoint Him or we are enjoying the sin a little too much and are not ready to let go. When you are close to God and you surrender yourself to him totally, He reveals the ugly parts of you and transforms you to be a more Christ-like being.

God is your counselor. He's the helper you need for your sinful addiction. When you are in a bind, call on Him to help you instead of hiding and continuing the same sin over and over again. Sin is not bigger than God. God is in you, therefore sin can never be bigger than you. Don't give it power over you.

God loves you. Give yourself over to Him and He will guide you and protect you in all facets of life. *Trust in the Lord with all your heart, And lean not on your own understanding; In all your ways acknowledge Him, And He shall direct your paths* (Proverbs 3:5, 6). Remember God loves you and He is on the throne!

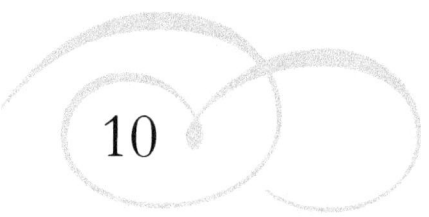

10

Self Examination is Absolutely Necessary

Examine yourselves as to whether you are in the faith. Test yourselves. Do you not know yourselves, that Jesus Christ is in you?—unless indeed you are disqualified (2 Corinthians 13:5).

Have you ever placed your hand over your heart and wondered what keeps your heart beating just as many others die around you? Why are you still alive when people die every day? As stressful and difficult as life may seem, do you ponder the beat of your heart and think of the day it will actually stop beating? Doctors face death every day, and sometimes I wonder if faced with all that death they go home and make their lives count. Are they determined to live fully and be happy at all costs because one day, just like their patients, it will be their turn to face death? I hope they do. When you are surrounded by death, you will gain a new appreciation for life, but it's more fulfilling when it's God-focused. Why? Because God created you and He created you for a purpose and He hopes you fulfill that purpose before your life ends. This is why He pursues you relentlessly, and unfortunately, the most effective way He gets your attention is to let you go through a season of drought. When all you know and love is taken from you and you are in a tight corner, you find yourself seeking answers. God has to break you in order to use you. He has to remove materialism and the shallow love of self from you in order for you to see Him clearly. You may have been a Christian for many years but suddenly in a season of drought you examine yourself and see you have a long way to go. You have barely started your Christian walk. Is God cruel? No way! The harder He tries to get your attention, the more He wants to use you for His glory so count it all joy.

Have you ever wondered what Jesus did for thirty years before He actually started His documented ministry? Can you imagine our Creator Himself coming to live amongst us? All the challenges He had to go through just as we do every day but knowing at any point He could call it off and play His royalty card? How many times did He have to hold His tongue from saying, "Do you know who I am? You are nothing without me. I could get rid of you right now if I wanted to!" Jesus humbled Himself and even let His creation overpower Him, humiliate Him and mistreat Him countless times because He was focused on the end goal and fulfilling His purpose. When Jesus was born, He was born in the flesh with all the attributes of the flesh just like we are. I believe He spent a lot of time in prayers and worked on subduing His flesh. He was born like us — selfish, angry, greedy, proud. He was born with every "flesh" characteristic you can think of, yet He prevailed. What am I saying to you? Do not glorify any man. Do not glorify your pastor or your spouse or your parents or your siblings or even your children. The flesh in us makes us fail, makes us fall. We have to subdue it and only through God can we subdue this flesh. It is a daily and a lifetime battle. Philippians 2:12 mentions working out your salvation with fear and trembling. Focus on your walk with Jesus Christ and how to be a better Christian and how to be a light wherever you are and how to show love wherever you are. Don't look to your pastor so that if he falls you wonder and condemn. If he falls, pray for him and show him love. Don't look to your husband or wife for validation. Look to God. Sharon Jaynes says in many of her books a "good husband makes a poor God". Even the best of husbands cannot fulfill his wife the only way God can. Neither can the president of the best wives club (if such a thing exists) fulfill her husband the only way God can. So never idolize and watch your pride too. *Therefore let him who thinks he stands take heed lest he fall* (1 Corinthians 10:12) Jesus is the only role model you should look unto when it comes to your Christian walk. No one else has perfected and prevailed over the flesh like He did so if you put anyone on a pedestal of perfection other than Jesus Christ you are in for a big disappointment.

There is a spiritual yearning in every man. God created it so we can find our way to Him. That's why there are so many religions in the world each believing theirs is the way. This is why Jesus had to clarify it for us, *Jesus said to him, "I am the way, the truth, and the life. No one comes to the Father except through Me* (John 14:6). When you begin to develop an intimate relationship with God, He will enlighten you on so many things. He will teach you true love, which is unconditional love, the love of Jesus Christ for us. He will teach you to focus on your heavenly goals. He will teach you to trust Him. In order to bring glory to God and live in His image we need to subdue our flesh. Have you seen two babies fight over a toy? It's in you to take when someone takes from you. It's in you to hurt right back when someone hurts you. But Christ says turn the other cheek (Luke 6:29). This doesn't make sense if you operate in the flesh, but if you operate in the spirit and you are focused on your eternity with God it makes a lot of sense. *And if your eye causes you to sin, pluck it out. It is better for you to enter the kingdom of God with one eye, rather than having two eyes, to be cast into hell fire—* (Mark 9:47) When you subdue your flesh, things of this world will begin to lose their hold over you. Things you placed so much importance in will stop being the priority. In Ecclesiastes 1:2 King Solomon with all his wisdom and riches and achievements declared it all vanity (meaningless, emptiness). So I ask you what you are trying to achieve on this earth, wealth? Climbing up the corporate ladder? Getting married? Having children? Being a world renowned athlete? Establishing civilization on another planet? Discovering the elusive fountain of youth? Whatever it is, is it worth putting your eternity with God at risk? When you achieve it, you will still be empty without Christ. *For what will it profit a man if he gains the whole world, and loses his own soul?* (Mark 8:36) Go and ask the rich and famous if they are content with their lives. The devil makes you always want more; meanwhile, time is going and you are not achieving anything for your Creator. Be the best you can be, but always prioritize God. Check yourself because one day your heart will stop beating and none of the things you have achieved on earth will go with you.

We are all guests in a hotel. We check in when we are born and check out when we die. We have no idea how long we will reside in the hotel. Are we making each day count? Some are privileged to know their check out time is imminent. If they are wise they put their houses in order, repent and prepare to meet their Maker. Many are not privileged to know their check out time. Many live in the hotel like it is their final resting place. God created us for His glory, He loves us and wants us to live for Him, but it is our choice. Choose God today, choose God always so when you check out you know you will be with Him. Make no mistake. He is not a God of compromise but a God of holiness and righteousness. So all the flashy and tempting things in the hotel that are strategically placed to draw you away from God, you will have to ask for His grace not to succumb. Anytime you find yourself in a gray area ask yourself, "Will this bring glory to God?" If you are tempted to react a certain way ask yourself, "Is this how God will react?" Remember God loves you and He is on the throne!

11

Seeds of Discontentment in Marriage

...Weeping may endure for a night, But joy comes in the morning (Psalm 30:5)

Seeds of discontentment are the devil's specialty. Time and time again, I come across women who are emotionally dissatisfied in their marriages. You want to know the crux of the problem? Face it, men and women are totally different. We look different physically, we feel things differently and we look at life differently. But God has determined we are good for each other. Also, you have to recognize that marriage is in seasons. Do you feel the same way about life in the summer as you do in the winter? I can tell you during winter time, I am more sluggish. I want to sleep more and I want to be cozy. Sometimes you miss that old feeling when you were living in the discovery of new found love and you and your spouse were all about each other in your own world. Marriage is the reality check to that feeling. Where before it may have been effortless, now you have to create time to ensure it doesn't get left behind. What happens? Children, financial stress, getting too comfortable and predictable with each other and a host of other things. When you were dating, your emotions as a woman were fed and full and you trusted this man with your heart and love. Perhaps you thought your emotions would always be full, but here you are today emotionally dissatisfied and unable to understand why you mention things over and over to your husband and he doesn't seem to get it. You have a choice to become a nag, and a bitter one at that, or to hide yourself in God's Word and understand that marriage is about selflessness. You are to love even when you feel unloved or taken for granted. You are to do your part even if it seems it's all for nothing. *Wives, likewise, be submissive to your own husbands, that even if some do not obey the word, they, without a word, may be won by the conduct of their wives* (1 Peter 3:1).

When you begin to reflect on your eternity and understand this world is your temporary home, you will do all you can to ensure you are pleasing God. And pleasing God is not easy because your "self" wants to repay hurt for hurt. For example, there are wives who tell their husbands to sleep on the couch because of minute things they may have done. Some decide since their husbands are not fulfilling them emotionally, stepping outside of the marriage to fill that void is a good idea. In truth it is a selfish act. That person who is making you feel good about yourself if you leave your husband for him you will find yourself back where you are trying to run away from. No one can keep that emotional high forever. If your husband started out giving you flowers on your birthday, it will get to a point that you wonder why he can't get you something else.

Romance evolves. Before it may have been chocolate and flowers, now with children him cooking Thanksgiving dinner may be more than enough to keep your emotional cup brimming.

When I watched Tyler Perry's *Temptation Confessions of a Marriage Counselor*, it broke down the doors of what emotional dissatisfaction can do. If you get a chance, please watch the movie. You start your life doing all the right things and all it takes is a whisper from the devil and suddenly you question all you have ever known. You wonder about the grass on the other side. I want you to know that there are snakes in all grass. Better you know where your snakes are and can easily navigate them than go to the other side and find out you are dealing with pythons and a variety of venomous snakes instead. Any issue you have with your spouse, take it to God so He can be the judge of the matter and resolve it in the manner that befits your home. Also ask God to remove certain desires in you so if your spouse never fulfills them, you will be more than okay. It is through those unfulfilled desires that the seeds of discontentment are sown by the devil. What seed is the devil sowing in your mind and heart today? This is his specialty. Don't give in but instead stand strong on God's Word. Marriage is a lot of things, but I personally believe it's also a master plan designed by God for you to make Heaven. Who on this earth will hurt you or drive you more crazy than your spouse and children? Where else can you truly learn unconditional love and forgiveness?

Matthew 5:8 says, *blessed are the pure in heart, for they shall see God.* When you love unconditionally and also forgive unconditionally, your heart will be pure. When your heart is pure, you will see God. You will see glimpses of God here on earth, but you will see Him in all His glory when you spend eternity with Him. Jesus spent a lot of time talking about love and forgiveness. He also lived it. This leads me to know both are crucial if you want to make Heaven. *And you shall love the Lord your God with all your heart, with all your soul, with all your mind, and with all your strength.' This is the first commandment. And the second, like it, is this: 'You shall love your neighbor as yourself.' There is no other commandment greater than these"* (Mark 12:30, 31). You can do everything right, but if you harden your heart you cannot get into a true relationship with God. Without a true relationship with God, the importance of forgiveness will bypass you. Matthew 18:21-22 says, *Then Peter came to Him and said, "Lord, how often shall my brother sin against me, and I forgive him? Up to seven times?" Jesus said to him, "I do not say to you, up to seven times, but up to seventy times seven.* The devil knows marriage is ordained by God to understand the truth of His Word and to live it daily. He fights it with seeds of discontentment, opens your eyes like when Adam and Eve ate the forbidden fruit so you can compare your spouse with others out there. Be careful! Understand the games of the devil and don't give in. Pray more and praise more. Learn to pray selfless prayers instead of asking God all the time to change your spouse ask Him to change... YOU!

The more you love God, the more every emotional void in you is filled by Him. Christian maturity gives you the fortitude to bear in all seasons. That's why marriage is for better and for worse. The worse will come a lot of times in your marriage. You have to make up your mind to stand on God's Word and please your Father in Heaven. Don't throw your marriage away on a selfish desire to live in that old feeling. If you are not married or even thinking of being married right now what evil seeds are taking root in you? Ask God to help you weed them out immediately. Do not compromise your faith and values for greener pastures. There's a price to pay when you dance with the devil. *There is a way that seems right to a man, But its end is the way of death* (Proverbs 16:25). God's love is free. Even when you are unloving, He still loves you. And His love has integrity because He sent His only and beloved son to die for you. The price has been paid there is no catch. The devil gives you all you want but his price is high. Don't mess with him. Seek to do God's will and please Him so He grants you peace and your eternity is not in jeopardy. Heaven and hell are very real! Love God, live for God.

It's not about how many Bible verses you can quote. Instead how many Bible verses are you actually living? It is with God's Word you can fight every evil thought the devil places in your mind. This is how Jesus Christ overcame temptation (Matthew 4:1-11). Meditate on God's Word and let it actually become a part of you. Let His Word become flesh in your life so you are able to withstand temptation, discontentment, and the evil strategies of the devil. God will hold your hand through all seasons of your marriage. He is the one that has joined you as man and wife. If you let go of Him, success will be like chasing the pot of gold at the end of the rainbow. Remember God loves you and He is on the throne!

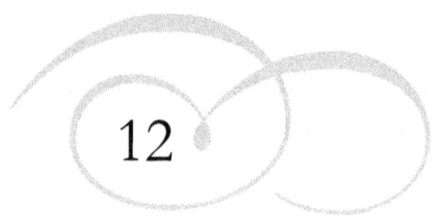

12

Do Your Words Edify?

Let no corrupt word proceed out of your mouth, but what is good for necessary edification, that it may impart grace to the hearers (Ephesians 4:29).

I have always been bothered by cuss words or foul language especially when used by fellow Christians. I remember back in high school when the boys talked loosely and freely I used to caution them to watch their language. And they learned to speak properly around me. Of course I was teased for it but I stood my ground and commanded their respect. Cuss words have always rubbed me the wrong way. Now I know it is the Spirit of God in me that repels the crude and distasteful language that is widely used in our society and people think is cool. I remember tuning in excitedly to watch a particular show but by the first commercial break the excitement was replaced by disappointment. Why? Almost every word out of the cast members was a cuss. I wondered to myself how they could keep an intelligent dialogue when almost every other word was crude and insulting. What many Christians lack is the fear of God. We do not address our bosses crudely in our work places yet when we get home we converse crudely forgetting God knows all and sees all.

There are some sinful acts we commit that we don't see as sin because it is the norm but I'm here to tell you, using foul language is a sin. The Word of God says so in Ephesians 4:29 cuss words are "unwholesome" another version says "corrupt" and they definitely do not "build others up" and I can assure you they do not "benefit" those who listen. God is our ultimate Father and He's not like our parents on earth we can hide he dark sides of our character from Sorry! He knows all about us and He knows whether we use cuss words or not. I am burdened to share this because a lot of Christians do not see this as a big deal. You may be struggling in this area or you may think you are doing nothing wrong but I hope you can decide to make a change today. We are Ambassadors of the Most High. The world watches us closely and we are supposed to be examples rather than succumbing to the vices of this world. Be so different that people will walk up to you and ask you what you have. It will be an opportunity to share your faith. Remember to be loving also. It is very important to show love, Christianity is love. Let's pray for ourselves and our brothers and sisters in Christ who struggle with carnality that we will truly have the fear of God. He will give us the wisdom to speak positively into lives and at the same time edify Him and bring glory to His name. *Let the words of my mouth and the meditation of my heart Be acceptable in Your sight, O Lord, my strength and my Redeemer.* (Psalms 19:14). Remember God loves you and He is on the throne!

Giving Your Life to Christ

This is the best decision you will ever make in life. You were created for God's glory and to keep His garden beautiful. Above all, He wants you to spend eternity with Him when you die. The only way to spending eternity with God in Heaven is to surrender your life to Him. If you have decided to, after reading this Holy Spirit inspired book then pray this simple prayer from your heart:

Lord Jesus, I come to you now to present myself. Today, I have come to truly believe that you are on your throne in Heaven and that you love me. I confess to you now that I am a sinner and I am not worth being considered to be associated with you. But you are truly a merciful God, who loves all. I therefore ask you humbly to forgive me all my sins and remember them no more from today. Please have mercy on me and forgive me. Cleanse me with your precious blood and make me a new person today. Thank you for doing this for me. I desire to follow you from today, serve you and obey your commandments as written in the scriptures. So help me Lord. From today, I make you my Savior, Master, and the Lord of my life. Thank you Lord Jesus, for giving me a new life. I pray in Jesus name. Amen.

Congratulations and welcome my new brother or sister in Christ. I will love to hear from you please email me: Beauty4ashes1230@aol.com.

God bless you forever and always.

Bella

ABOUT THE AUTHOR

Bella Alex-Nosagie is God's Handmaiden sent to remind people in this generation whose love has "waxed cold" (Matthew 24:12) that God's love is steadfast and has the power to resurrect everything that is dead in you and around you. She is the Founder of Beauty4Ashes12:30 Publishing, LLC, a writing ministry that spreads the good news of God's unconditional love to all across the globe.

Bella received her college degree in Speech Communication from The University of Georgia in Athens, Georgia, U.S.A. before moving into corporate America and rose to the position of Global Project Manager liaising with Pharmaceutical Companies. Bella is an ordained Minister of God and is also the author of, *Woman in Crisis: Overcoming the Devastation of Marital Disappointment*. Bella is married and blessed with two beautiful children and resides with her family in the United States.

Bella is always honored to hear from her readers. You can contact her directly at beauty4ashes1230@aol.com.

To learn more about Bella Alex-Nosagie and her ministry visit www.beauty4ashes1230.org.

www.ingramcontent.com/pod-product-compliance
Lightning Source LLC
Chambersburg PA
CBHW071716040426
42446CB00011B/2086